Care
at the
Core

Conversational Essays on Identity, Education and Power

Sherri Spelic

Care at the Core
Sherri Spelic

Design: Monica C. LoCascio of MAKE BOOKS HAPPEN
& Sebastian Kaltenbrunner

Photography: Alexandra Thompson

2nd Edition, October 2019

Publisher: tredition GmbH,
Halenreie 40-44, 22359 Hamburg, Germany

For Noah and James

Contents

Introduction

Books and Conversation; Books as Conversations

I love books probably because my mother loved books and I wanted to be like her even without ever openly admitting it. Our house was stuffed with books and other reading material from the basement to the attic. Although I don't recall ever describing myself as a bookworm, I know that I enjoyed being read to as a child and later took pleasure in choosing my own books to read. Once at an admissions interview for 9th grade, I remember the adult across from me suggested that I must be quite a reader based on whatever evidence he had in front of him. I was kind of stumped because I didn't identify that way. In retrospect, I wonder if reading was such a given that I could never see it as anything outstanding or special.

Reading is what we did in our household just like watching TV or listening to music or talking on the phone. Wherever we might sit for longer than a few minutes in the kitchen or living room, something to read—Sunday's newspaper, *Jet* and *Ebony* magazines, a cookbook, a paperback novel—was always within reach. People who visited our house would pick up a paper or book and leaf through it while talking to my mom. When I look at my own home now, I see that my mother's legacy is very much in effect. One needn't go far in our apartment to find a book or magazine to read. My own bookshelves are full and line a wall. My younger son's collection of picture books needs weeding to create space for the next wave of chapter books. My husband's shelves are beginning to require more creative stacking methods to accommodate his growing collection of non-fiction. Although my oldest has been living on his own for several years, a substantial stash of Japanese manga titles remain in our backroom storage and has recently become a treasure trove for his little brother.

I come from a family of book lovers and aim to further the inheritance. All good.

But what is all this accumulation good for? Why stacks upon stacks of books both read and unread? Not every book added to the collection has been or will be read. There are no guarantees or contracts, nor do I keep any sort of reading log to indicate any book's consumption status. One of my private joys is looking at a book on a shelf or in a stack and knowing if I've read it and if so, how much. Or perhaps I can at least recall how, when and why I acquired it. In this way books become markers of my life in progress; signposts that remind me where I've been and what I've chosen to think about. Behold the beauty of books: their stasis and solidity! Once published, printed, distributed and purchased (or given away) books lead their own lives in the hands and minds of readers. Many may never make it that far, however. But that should deter none of us from attempting to toss one more (or even many more) tomes onto the pile of written history.

In deciding to write a book, I acknowledge my intention to create a concrete thing that will last. A thing that will collect dust and perhaps be forgotten but I will have made it and left it as a container of words and thoughts I wanted you to hear and remember before I go. In offering you a book, I present you with my personally crafted signpost for your journey; an artifact of time we can spend together.

Among the many books on my shelves, I have a slim little volume by Mexican author, Gabriel Zaid, who speaks directly to the joys and also dilemmas of *So Many Books*[1]:

> "The reading of books is growing arithmetically; the writing of books is growing exponentially. If our passion for writing goes unchecked, in the near future there will be more people writing books than reading them."

That said, Zaid offers us some comfort in acknowledging that it is ultimately our tremendous diversity as readers that will accommodate this tip in the scales between writing and reading. He reminds us:

> "Reading liberates the reader and transports him to participate in conversations, and in some cases to arrange them, as so many active readers do: parents, teachers, friends, writers, translators, critics, publishers, booksellers, librarians.
>
> The uniqueness of each reader, reflected in the particular nature of his personal library (his intellectual genome), flourishes in diversity. And the conversation continues, between the excesses of commerce, between the sprawl of chaos and the concentration of the market." *(So Many Books, p. 10-11)*

---

1 Gabriel Zaid, *So Many Books: Reading and Publishing in an Age of Abundance*. London: Sort of. 2004.

Precisely his use of the term "conversation" captures so well my ambition and desire in compiling this collection of blog posts and articles that I have published over the last 5 or 6 years. Each slice of writing amplifies conversations I want or need to have. Conversations with other writers, educators, learners, students, loved ones; people I admire as well as with people who confound me. Writing has turned out to be my most effective means to process what I read, hear and experience. Every conversation exposes the ongoing volley of ideas within as I try my best to understand and make sense of the world around me.

To create a book of previously published online material marks my deliberate attempt to press pause in the daily churn of digital output. Even as I write these words digitally, I periodically dip into Twitter and e-mail. I know that the way I sit with a book (yes, the print version) is different from how I behave in front of a screen. My attention flows differently. I have distractions when I read a book but my custom is to let those distractions rise, fall and pass as opposed to jumping screens to gawk in response to whatever has chimed or popped up in a new tab. One of my regrets with online engagement is how hard it can feel to slow down, stop even, and really spend time with a text and let it work on you for a while. Hot takes on the latest out-rage are often so fast and furious (in every sense of the word) that in our rush to keep up, we no longer allow ideas to ripen, mature or perhaps even shift their original shape.

The posts I've selected here reflect a true cross-section of my online writing. The book is divided into sections which serve as very broad topic umbrellas: Identifying, Writing, Sharing, Observing Education and Everything Else with a couple of in-terludes in between. The posts in each section appear, more or less chronologically. That said, there is no requirement to read these posts or sections in the order in which they appear. On the contrary, read what calls to you at any given time. Rather than a sit-down meal of several courses, consider this collection an all-you-can-read buffet for which you have as much time as you can spare.

I invite you to take a meandering walk with me through the words and thoughts of many others—of my students, colleagues, friends and perfect strangers. Let's consider what we read and how we interpret what we read. Dig in with a teaspoon or a shovel. Whatever you discover and value here is bound to be unique to you. In this way, this book becomes one of yours and no longer entirely mine. It joins your stacks and leaves mine. This is the beauty of the conversation we can continue.

Identifying

CHAPTER I

Can I get a witness?

On Identity Writing

When I was young, I was itching for a career on the stage. I thought dance or acting would be my domain. I took ballet and loved it. As a tween, I built up a tidy repertoire of comic reproductions of TV ads that my classmates would beg me to repeat over and over again. (My best imitation was of the York Peppermint Patty ad[2] which featured a Black woman office worker describing rapture at first bite.) In those moments I felt successful, like I was reaching my audience. Later on, in high school and college, I spent more time on athletic pursuits where I got to shine a little, particularly on the track.

All things considered, I did well. I attended my first choice college and had the opportunity to study abroad which dramatically changed my life's geographical trajectory. For the most part, I have been able to spend my academic and professional time among people who rarely looked like me but with whom I shared a sense of belonging. I am accustomed to fitting in because it is what I do: I observe, I imitate, I blend in. I learned to fit the bill, even if it changes.

---

2 https://www.youtube.com/watch?v=179kmvQZtEM

My career on the stage never came to pass. Like certain articles of clothing, I outgrew my childhood dream of fame. Instead, I became a teacher and coach using my flair for the dramatic to grab and hold students' fleeting attention while convincing the skeptics that the goods I'm selling (i.e., better skills and fitness) are worth their time and effort. Among friends and at home, I take pleasure in being a good listener; reliable, robust and flexible.

Then came blogging and social media, followers and readers, and slowly I had an audience. Numerically modest but important to me, there were and are people who read what I write: a blog post, thread of tweets, a comment. This experience of being public—of sharing my thoughts with whoever finds them—has given me pause on several occasions. My increased use of "I" in the public domain has regularly forced me to confront the many layers of that singular pronoun.

The essays that follow offer varied attempts at unpacking the contents of "I" when writing. While finding words to comprehend and situate my identity I often wrestled with experiences of (in)visibility as a Black woman. I had to ask myself what it means to be seen, by whom, and on what that depends. Identity also covers the ways I present myself in social contexts: the rules I adhere to as well as the ones I snub. Challenging myself to describe the figure who emerges when I look at my interests, achievements and concerns stretched me in new ways. The question: "what is true?" complicated and clarified my process. It seems like every time I think I know who I am, I discover new truths about myself. I become a witness to my own unfolding.

My pre-teen comedic self was desperate to capture the rapt attention of my peers, if only for a moment. Perhaps even then I already understood what an accomplishment that was for a skinny Black girl surrounded by mostly white classmates. To confirm that I was more than an apparition, I needed to attract a bevy of witnesses. To assure myself that even if I was not of them, I could count myself somehow among them. Writing my identity beckons more witnesses to the spectacle of this life in progress. I hold up a mirror for myself and find that I am not as alone as I feared.

CHAPTER II

Am I a #PhysEd Teacher?

March 20th, 2014

That's an identity question. And it would appear to be easily answerable.

Am I or am I not a #PhysEd teacher?

Not surprisingly, my response is a "Yes, and..."

Because if you examine my social media profiles, you might have to dig a little deeper to locate that particular identifier.

On LinkedIn you get: Professional Leadership Coach.

On Twitter you'll find:

Leadership Coach, Educator, Workshop designer and facilitator, avid reader & writer @ home on the edge of the alps. #100Connections

Facebook: Don't even bother.

So, clearly I'm not advertising my Physical Education badge. Hmmm...

Rather, I choose to identify as an educator. That's broad, comprehensive and some might say, vague, too. I'll agree to all of those.

Yet what brought me to social media were broader interests than what goes on in PE. I came to find insights on education as an industry, as a public and private good, as a right, as a privilege, as a vehicle, as a force. I wanted to think more deeply about learning as a habit, as an opportunity, as a chore, as a moving target. I was looking to challenge my understanding of teaching as a practice, a career, a stepping stone, as an absolute.

And yes, I am a #PhysEd teacher.

When I am in the gym with students, I am at home. I have music playing, I am moving around correcting body positions ("side to target") or issuing reminders ("What does that mean: '*to* your partner'?"). The day is flush with groups coming and going, with grade level transitions to make your head spin (i.e., from 5th to KG) and I love all that. I've been at it for over 20 years and have been blessed to work with an incredible bunch of colleagues who not only know their stuff but keep adding to and improving their "stuff."

The advantages of being a physical educator are many beyond the surface ones that everyone likes to put out there: comfortable clothing (all day, every day) and no papers to grade. What I prize and what keeps me coming back are the special relationships I can develop with students. Because we're working with the body which is a very concrete and immediate experience, I encounter each child's vulnerability and unique strengths in very different ways than a classroom teacher might.

In the course of a school year, I see every child struggle with something. Every one of them has something, some barrier they need to overcome. For some, it may be social—finding and working with partners. For others, there may a particular area of movement that proves challenging or even frightening. My job is to facilitate each child's struggles towards a positive outcome for that individual within our class group framework. The gym provides fertile soil for cultivating a growth mindset in every child and in this teacher.

Yes, I am a #physicaleducator who believes that all educators need to be ready to learn from their students, their colleagues, parents, and countless other educators who are eager to share and dialogue. I am out to learn for more than myself and to do that effectively, I cannot and will not simply "stay in my lane." On the contrary, I travel off-road cross country and consider myself an all-terrain learner. And in the process, I am making tracks, leaving impressions, having an impact.

No sleeping on this job.

Yes, I am a #physical educator and all of my work is about moving: moving minds, moving hearts, moving bodies.

CHAPTER III

What I Will Fret Over

April 25, 2014

I spend quite a bit of time thinking about education. I also think, write and talk a lot about school, schools and schooling. I am a teacher. I am an educator. I am a coach. I am a parent. Not so long ago an idea reached me that offered surprising clarity: On my deathbed I will not be wishing I had fret more over my children's education.

> On my deathbed I will not be wishing I had fret more over my children's education.

Rather, when that day arrives I may fret about their futures. About whether they know how much I love them. I will hope that they know how rich they have made my life. I will hope that they understand themselves to be capable and extraordinary human beings. I will pray that they have learned to trust others, how to reach out for help, how to care for and love others especially when loving is hard to do. I will fret that we have not had enough time to say all the things that we wanted to say to each other. I will fret over whether their passion for life and learning will be enough to see them through, in and on whatever paths they pursue. It is extremely unlikely that I will fret over how they did or are doing in school.

I have two sons: the firstborn is of age and can decide what kind of learning he would like to pursue and if that involves more formal schooling and a second who is at the beginning of his grade school career. So the question arises: If I know that I will not wish I had fret more over their school experience when my life is at its end, what does that mean for now?

It means that my eyes must be on the larger prize, even as my children go through school and further their education, year after year. It means that my most urgent purpose is to nurture the relationships which will sustain them for life. And that means not only their relationships to people. I must carefully attend to their relationships to learning as a joy, an avenue, a journey and a foundation. I need to actively cultivate their relationships to the world of ideas, to the literacy and curiosity that this demands, to the arts in myriad forms, to the vast diversity of this earth we inhabit. I need to foster and champion their relationships to their unique strengths, interests and passions — providing them with evidence and experience that says, "this counts and is important to who you are and wish to be."

And knowing full well that I will likely fall short of these lofty goals in small and larger ways, it becomes all the more crucial that I persist in reading to them night after night, day after day. That I continue to listen to their stories of adventure, danger, humor and drama drawn from the screen, the playground, the last good book or video game. That I watch them play outdoors, indoors, with friends, alone, on a PC, on a tablet. That we talk about what was scary or sad or disappointing or awesome. That I pay attention to their wishes as well as to their disdain. That I learn from them and allow them to instruct me. One goes to school and the other may be done with school; Homework is something they both know can be done, forgotten or ignored. What happened at school is sometimes newsworthy, other times less so. Our connections to each other are what matter now and throughout our journey. That is where my energy flows first and foremost.

When I extend this thinking from my sons to include my students and athletes, I arrive at similar conclusions. Whether or not they recall how to stand at bat or how to pass a soccer ball is not the ultimate point of my instruction. Rather, in how many ways can they learn to appreciate their unique bodies and capabilities? What are the things they look forward to doing with their bodies and minds in school, after school, in life? If they have cause to remember me at all as their teacher, let it be as someone who enjoyed sharing her enthusiasm for movement and people and community. Let them remember when and how they felt proud of themselves in Physical Education or on the track. Let them remember that movement was fun and challenging and something they kept doing ever after because they chose to do it. The relationships that we build, teacher-student, student-student, as well as the connection of students and teacher to the subject matter—can be such powerful sources of change, growth, and genuine education.

When it is time for us to leave this life behind, today's piling on of curricular rigor will not save us or our children. What will make a positive difference, *the* positive difference, are the deliberately individual loving and caring relationships we build not only among the human parties involved but with the world as a limitless learning environment. Shaping, cultivating, harvesting and preserving the multiple learning landscapes we inhabit—this is the opportunity we share as teachers, as parents, as students, as learners and survivors to make our time together on this earth meaningful and worthy.

CHAPTER IV

Woman. Black. Fit. Angry. (In)visible. All of the above.

August 7th, 2015

Two essays this week caught me unawares and have left me restless in their wake. The first is "Yes, I Am An Angry Black Woman" by Stacey Patton, published in *DAME* magazine [3] and the second is "Fitted" by Moira Weigel in *The New Inquiry* [4]. While it is easier to guess the thrust of the first essay based on the title, the second is less overt. Weigel talks about the rise of FitBit and other activity trackers and their association with a whole new brand of female productivity. Both of these essays spoke to me in significant ways. And their separateness from each other presents me with an internal dilemma I hope to solve by writing about it now.

---

3 Stacey Patton, "Yes, I'm The Angry Black Woman" in *Dame Magazine*, Aug. 3, 2015 http://www.damemagazine.com/2015/08/03/yes-im-angry-black-woman#sthash.jbKFgqre.dpuf

4 Moira Weigl, "Fitted" in *The New Inquiry*, July 27, 2015. https://thenewinquiry.com/fitted/

First of all, I encourage you to read Stacey Patton's stirring call to attention, whoever you are. With her words, she invites the reader to inhabit her simmering state of mind in all its complexity, fervor and power. On the day after the Charleston Massacre she describes her ride on an East Coast train:

> ...The news of Charleston was difficult to process, even more so while riding a D.C.-bound train packed with White people, most of them dressed in business attire, who seemed oblivious to the tragedy. It took everything I had in me to keep from erupting with rage in that Amtrak car.
>
> I thought about racial terrorism and its larger history while a nearby White woman worked on a New York Times crossword puzzle, and sipped her Starbucks coffee. I raged thinking how not even churches are safe from the pathologies of White supremacy. Others talked on their cell phones about trivial shit or tapped on their laptop keyboards and tablets.
>
> It was clear I was not among friends or a community that shared my sadness, anger, or angst about what it means to be Black in America in the 21st century. A pair of women sitting behind me chatted and laughed loudly. They were free of worry, they were fearless and enjoying their privilege to live, to exist apart from the horrors of racial violence. Their joy made me resentful. Fighting waves of grief and tears of sorrow, I got up to change seats to get away from the noise of White privilege.

"The noise of white privilege." yeah, that landed.

Patton goes on to describe the historical roots of the Angry Black Woman stereotype. And this stereotype, while familiar to me, is the very one I have sought so carefully to avoid. Although

I have a temper and can get loud, this tends to happen within the safe confines of my own four walls among family, where I'm allowed to be just angry me—minus the socio-political layering. In my professional life and among friends, few would readily identify me as 'that angry Black woman.' And yet I know and feel the anger about which Stacey Patton speaks.

> Far too long, we have been fighting to dispel the Angry Black woman stereotype. But that's not the solution because the truth is, we are angry. Our rage is righteous. Our ire is understandable. Yet our anger is misunderstood.

And she makes the brave suggestion that we learn to see our rage as a creative power for change:

> Let's stop viewing our anger as a negative and appreciate it as a gift. Neuroscientists' research reveals that anger is a powerful means of social communication, and a natural part of any person's emotional resources. Anger helps us reach our goals, allowing us to be more optimistic, creative, and to solve problems. Anger is a source of fuel for motivating us to meet life's challenges and persuade others to do the right thing.

It's at this point in the essay where I get on my feet and start to wave my hands: "Yaaaasss!"

She closes with this:

> To feel our anger at injustice is to be wholly alive. Our ability and willingness to express that anger, is to be committed to progress. To wield our anger strategically is the key to the justice and freedom. And to fully embrace our anger is the most healthy, sane, self-loving, nurturing thing that we can possibly do.

"To feel our anger at injustice is to be wholly alive" provides a frame for why I engage here at all. It's not always because

I am angry, but often enough I am astonished, flabbergasted or amazed at the injustices we tolerate and let pass without addressing the root causes. There is plenty to be up in arms about—channeling that energy to agitate and push for change is what movements are made of. Stacey Patton's statements remind me that I may have to let go of the need to put on my happy face when I decide to engage for change outside of my precious four walls.

And then there's this second essay, "Fitted" which after "Yes, I Am An Angry Black Woman" reads a bit like "the noise of White privilege." Moira Weigel, however, expertly describes both the allure and burden of embedding 24/7 activity tracking in her own and other women's daily lives. She talks about the act of tracking emerging like a new, fully personalized religion. The sharing of one's most intimate data regarding movement, food intake, sleep and even sex in pursuit of constant improvement becomes the new vehicle towards salvation. The desire to not just be better but to also show off your new "better" is fueled by competing and commiserating with fellow activity trackers. While I consider myself a modest fitness enthusiast, this more recent trend of constant self-monitoring remains foreign to me even if I can understand the various motivations behind it.

All of these elements tied up with our cultural notions of what fit femininity looks like and how it is assessed in the current media climate made the essay a deeply compelling read for me. And as I read and re-read the essay I was struck by how very white it all feels. Even if I know that FitBit users come in all colors, shapes and sizes, the folks who best conform to Weigel's distinctive portrayal strike me as most likely to be White, straight, upper middle-class women. After describing the new beauty/fitness ideal of our times as exorexic, she clues us in as to how this movement trend is likely to play out in practical and ideological terms:

Today, the ideal woman is exorexic.

In Ancient Greek, orexis means "desire" or "appetite." The prefix an means "not." A true anorexic wants nothing. Ex is Latin, for "out of"; arcere means "restrain." "Exercise" meant to break out of what is holding you, and to push the limit. The exorexic craves a challenge. Specifically, she aims to work her way out of desiring itself. ...

Today, the exorexic eroticizes work itself. The army of women in Lululemons and Nike Frees who bound purposefully along the sidewalks of more and more American cities proclaim no specific taste, but rather an insatiable appetite for effort. They wear the uniform of an upper middle class for whom the difference between leisure and work is supposed to have disappeared.

Do what you love and you will never work a day in your life. When the guidance counselors say this, they suggest that if you work, you will be loved — or at least deserve love. Make yourself lovable first, they say, and sure as day you can trade that strange coin, ability, in for happiness later. They do not tell you the principle that follows. Love work above all and you will never rest.

Granted, I am enamored of this particular passage. Weigel's subjects present themselves vividly in my imagination: they are ambitious, well-educated, weight conscious and (to my mind) oh so very white. These are some of those same women who go on to become helicopter perfectionist parents, I suppose. (Cliché I realize, but irresistibly so.) I, too, am ambitious, well-educated and weight conscious. I enjoy feeling productive and disciplined and operate much better in the world when those two characteristics are visible. The plot thickens, however, when I consider that my white sisters' ambition and effort will be judged and assessed quite differently from mine based primarily on well-worn yet invisible unconscious bias.

As a Black woman, my work is consistently cut out for me. The way the world tends to view my effort and the body I produce with that same effort is likely to be perceived differently than those of Weigel's "army of women". My muscles have often been interpreted as defying femininity. I get to be "strong" but not "pretty". I am good at my job; yet to advance beyond my current status can seem more like a mountain to climb rather than the logical next step it might be for an equally educated and experienced candidate from the dominant group. This realization has been decades in the making: It's not just me and my personal inadequacies, there are systemic factors at play. Being female and Black pose barriers that I previously did not wish to acknowledge. And my identification with and understanding of the dominant group's ways of being and functioning help and hinder me in unique ways.

Weigel sums up the significance of the FitBit mania for her particular demographic in the following way:

> FitBit users remain, above all, productive, in our data and our visibility. We do not succumb to that wan, sick decadence, the aggressively infertile unproductivity of the true anorexic. This is female labor becoming frictionless. The point of the game is to just not disappear.

That's it! That's the critical difference I have struggled to name. For Weigel's exorexic women "the point of the game is to just not disappear." Of course! Weigel's "army of women" is highly visible. They are prominent, ubiquitous — seen everywhere you look from screens to billboards, to print media; in the majority of our retail spaces. For me in my Black female physicality and intellect, the point (and the struggle) is to *appear, to become visible, to cease being invisible.*

Aye, there's the rub! To be a Black woman in majority white spaces so easily becomes a form of invisibility: either in the way that we bend over backwards to assimilate into the dominant culture and its going narratives, or we stand out through our behavior or appearance which become the excuse for whites to look the other way and ignore our very presence. This feels like a revelation. This is where my path diverges from Weigel's hyper-productive women and draws me into Patton's harbor of validation and understanding.

In my struggle to be seen for all that I am, for all that I offer—I face barriers that are not of my own creation. The workarounds, passwords and gatekeeper relations I develop are original and unique to me. Both Weigel and Patton offer me insights to both the world that I inhabit and *the world that I am*. Both authors open my eyes to fresh perspectives and for that I feel deeply grateful.

For the record: I am Black. I am a woman. Sometimes I am angry. I am fit. I am an educator. I am a coach. I am a runner. I am a parent. I am a reader, writer, thinker, listener, observer. And more. Always more.

CHAPTER V

Alright, fine.

On Always Arriving at a Black Identity

March 19, 2017

My father had a standard line of approval he delivered for every imaginable celebration. Whether at Christmas, Easter, anniversary, or birthday, after receiving any kind of gift he would say, "Well, that's alright" with a soft chuckle. This phrase remains with me like a mental totem; those few words echoing the reassuring stability of my childhood.

As a parent, I have held onto that phrase and created my own predictable message which my husband suggests might make a good epitaph: "It/they/we will be fine." More reassurance in hopes of continued stability. 'Alright' and 'fine' —words I use to claim my faith: Faith in people, in a higher being, in the grandeur of the universe, in my family, in myself. In my heart of hearts, I am a believer.

Middle age prods me to look back more often now to see not only what I've done but also where I've come from. The way I see my parents now and appreciate their incredible sacrifices on my behalf and that of my siblings is fundamentally different from 15 or even 10 years ago. I loved them when they were still

"Well, that's alright." -Ancient African-American Proverb used by my dad

alive and now I pray to be blessed with even a fraction of their wisdom and fortitude.

Recently I found myself put out by something that I read. It was an in-depth run down on a billionaire eccentric [5] who exerts, along with several family members, an outsized degree of influence on the current US presidential administration. This was not the first such article [6] I had read about this individual.

5　"The Reclusive Hedge Fund Tycoon Behind Trump's Presidency, by Jane Mayer, March 27, 2017 *New Yorker Magazine*.

6　"Robert Mercer: the big data billionaire waging war on mainstream media" , by Carole Cadwalladr, Feb. 26, 2017, *The Guardian*.

What angered me, besides the awfulness he finances through huge donations, was acknowledging that he is just one of several. He happens to be the top money dog in DC currently but there are others who eagerly use their cash to ensure policy which favors their accumulating fortunes. And I keep having to read about them and what they support, to whom they have ties and witness in reality how very little concern and respect they have for their country and the citizens whose interests they (sometimes) claim to want to represent.

Clearly I am suffering from too much hyper *enriched* white bread in my media diet. The detailed biographies of so many wealthy power-wielding men with some deeply disturbing ideas about how the US ought to be run (or run aground) tend to leave me weighted down, blocked, lethargic. They knock the wind out of my resistance sails. They remind me that the future will not be new for marginalized people. It will hark back and draw strength from a long, dark and perpetually racialized American past. For every detail that I read about the billionaire family dynamics, kooky investments and attraction to conspiracy theories, both you and I know that this is never a two-way street. This is the antithesis of reciprocal interest or understanding. If the billionaire sponsors of the current administration ever seek to investigate or document anything about marginalized people it is and will be to confirm their own biases and reinforce their firmly held stereotypes and assumptions. And then develop policy accordingly. This angers me. [7]

However, recognizing this sequence of reporting and my consumption of it as part of a deeper, larger, more insidious pattern in my life, particularly as a Black woman has helped break the cycle of deflation. A brilliant thread [8] offered by @absurdistwords on Twitter allowed me to see myself in the

---

7 https://edifiedlistener.blog/2017/03/01/not-another-think-piece/

8 https://twitter.com/absurdistwords/status/841266425432006656

systems I've been struggling to escape. Essentially, his string of tweets put me in touch with a lifetime reality I had not yet fully acknowledged:

As a Black person, growing up and living in the United States, it was necessary and essential that I understand as much as possible about white people and their priorities in all sectors of society. While white involvement with and understanding of Black people, of me, remained primarily optional.

> "To not understand how white people work and think as a black person is to be fundamentally unequipped for life in America.
>
> On the other hand, as a white person you need to know absolutely nothing about black people to get through your day.
>
> Black people know white people better than they know themselves. White people tasked us with this from the beginning." — *@absurdistwords, 5'7 Black Male (Tweets Mar. 13, 2017)*

Both difficulty and advantage, understanding white people was a life lesson I was able to run with and cultivate, fine-tune and personify. For the whole of my school career, I was told by neighborhood Blacks that I "talked like a white girl." Predominately white institutions became my most consistent milieu away from home and remain so to this day. I relate easily to white people because I have spent so much of my life in their company. And while they are background-diverse, boasting various mixes of European extraction with occasional dabs of Middle Eastern, Asian or even African ancestry, their whiteness is salient even if they are oblivious to it. In contrast, I am visibly Black, like, no mistaking, definitely Black. That is salient for me wherever I go.

At the same time, I have doubted my capacity to be the right kind of Black woman, fulfilling both the Black and woman parts with equal success. I suppose this is the conundrum of identity each of us faces in unique ways: being all the pieces at once. And the layers of our education at home, school, in our communities and workplaces, these shape and complicate matters further.

My life's work may be to unravel the threads of my identity in a way that allows me to be all of who I am in all the contexts I inhabit. To that end, I have to make an extra effort to see myself because the worlds I walk in offer no approximate mirroring. I want to observe how I protect white friends and loved ones from having to struggle over topics of race; notice how readily I trust mainstream media narratives about my identity group, or how often I skip an opportunity to learn the history of my parents and grandparents in favor of learning more mainstream (white) historical narratives. This unfolding of approaches to becoming who I am provides a necessary antidote to the burden of being an inevitable scholar of white ways.

What fascinates me at 50 plus is the remarkable benefit of the longer view. I have reached an age where my presence at funerals is more likely than at weddings or baby showers. I am grandmother-eligible. I am on my way to becoming a Black elder. And I must ask myself: What kind of elder do I intend to be? What will I do to make the world better before I go? And as a Black elder, what is my responsibility to the young Black and brown women who will come after me? How do I raise my young men to be the feminists the world requires? There are no easy answers. So I read and ruminate and write.

Thoughts of legacy and mortality influence not only what I read, but *how*. As liberal democracies around the world struggle to maintain their electoral legitimacy, my need to grasp the threads of history that have led us to this point is great. As anti-Black racism and other forms of outright bigotry experience a click-inducing upswing in popularity, I seek out the voices of those most deeply and immediately affected. Witnessing egregious twists away from democratic norms and humane treatment of the most vulnerable requires that I place trust in those journalists, authors, and activists who will tell us what mainstream media will not. With my age and experience, I investigate our world with curious eyes that have seen some things, but remain blind to others. I read, learn, reflect and discuss in service of nudging us all forward. I connect my hard-won wisdom to that of writers and artists, past and present. My mortality is certain. My legacy can still be fashioned.

In the current political climate, it feels hard to believe that things are going to be alright. Survival is something you and I build together. As we age we can also open and welcome and grow. That's what I'm banking on. These will become my middle age superpowers. My parents would be proud. My dad would say, "Well, that's alright."

Deep appreciation to @absurdistwords for his tweet threads which provoked all kinds of reflection, some of which ended up in this post.

CHAPTER VI

Listening As Resistance

June 25, 2018

Here are some things I know about listening: It is a choice. It's a skill that requires practice. Most people believe they are better at it than they actually are. The act of listening involves more than hearing sounds; it requires thinking and feeling in order to be effective in communicating with others.

What I have learned about listening is that it is hard to contain our emotional reactivity if we don't like the message we're receiving. How well or how poorly we listen often reflects the value we place on the messenger in a given context. I can also listen as I read: listen to the characters and the author; allow their voices to reach me.

My Twitter and blogging handle is edifiedlistener. A name I thought up, claimed and that felt right. After 6 years at that digital address, in that digital identity, I still feel strongly about listening and am often edified by the act of careful, thoughtful listening with others. In the wake of more unsettling news from my home country, I find myself thinking about my listening choices and what really matters.

On most days I have the privilege of being able to hear and listen to a variety of people. I catch the headline news on Austrian national radio, I dip into my Twitter feed to hear from hundreds of people and organizations about happenings in the world, in homes, in schools, in mainstream media, and plenty of other places. This means I have to make choices. I have to decide to whom I will listen, which stories I will investigate further and reach conclusions about what these stories may mean for the people and issues I care about. This post is about how I reach some of the choices I do and what that's good for.

Online I belong to a few communities, many of which overlap and intersect. I keep up with other K-12 educators and Physical Education specialists. Higher Education professionals have welcomed me into their conversations on a variety of topics and I have learned from their diverse areas of expertise. Various entry points to Black Twitter have offered me sustenance on too many levels to count while more specific groups such as edtech bloggers of color or English teachers challenging the cannon with #DisruptTexts have afforded me opportunities to engage in areas of interest that are not in my designated academic wheelhouse. Finding people who know more about a given topic than I do is not hard. My buffet of options is nearly limitless.

The folks I seek out for their insights or leads offer more than their smarts, however. **I listen to people who have skin in the game.** If I'm wondering about education policy, then I'm going to listen to teachers who are tasked with implementing that policy. When the next political outrage floods my Twitter feed—then I'm going to turn my ear past mainstream media and listen up for what trusted voices on Black Twitter are saying. Why? Because I trust people who have been traditionally marginalized to have a perspective that does more than parrot what the holders of power are broadcasting. When corporate PR spreads their blanket assurances of wanting to serve customers best and needing to collect every imaginable data point in order to do that, then I listen to the capitalism and tech skeptics who can show me where the untruths are buried—whether in a company's Terms of Service, in its abysmal record of hiring for diversity, or elsewhere.

As we watch democratic norms in the United States steadily being eroded by an openly corrupt and destructive federal administration, **I'm listening acutely especially to women**, (Sarah Kendzior, Hend Amry, Leah McElrath, and Tressie McMillan Cottom) **who warned us before the election of 2016 and before the inauguration about what would follow.** Their voices have been fierce, unwavering and well informed. But the listening they have received seems remarkably weak in relation to the consistent accuracy of their claims.

My own capacity to listen widely, generously and attentively becomes my resistance.

I'm not gonna lie. I am definitely overwhelmed with the current political climate in the US and in Europe. Each further step to the right—that seeks to punish asylum seekers[9] rather than assist them, that reinforces racist policies under the guise of promoting national security, that proclaim dramatic cuts to welfare, health insurance, and public education to be inevitable and call for further privatization —each presents a new devastation in its own right. And as these devastations pile up, become normalized, and their arrivals accelerated, my own

---

9   "An Immigration Attorney on What It's Like to Represent Small Children Taken from Their Parents" by Alexandra Schwartz, June 19, 2018, *The New Yorker Magazine*.

capacity to sit and listen, to stand and listen, *to take the time to listen*, will be at risk.

If I am edified through listening, I am also, more than ever, tested in both. To "be uplifted, morally or spiritually; enlightened, informed [10]": edified is my goal. To remain a careful, patient and critical listener is still my calling. My capacity to listen widely, generously and attentively becomes my resistance. **In listening to learn I gather and process the information that allows me to contribute meaningfully to conversations.** That means while I read the updates on awful immigration policy developments, I continue to read about how automating public services to the poor sets the scene for a widening surveillance state [11] and why we need to show more concern and awareness than we currently are. As I parcel out my protest in tweets and retweets, I also dig into an academic text which explains in reasonable detail how liberal democracies can devolve into autocratic rule through legal means [12].

Listening as resistance also means that those communities to which I belong accept the fact that I will keep moving in several lanes at once; that I will not limit myself to one niche field of interest. My focus is trained on building political awareness more than social capital. Because if I'm honest, my life and that of my children depends on maintaining and bolstering an acute political awareness. If we want to live in a free society, I am learning that this requires fighting to defend those freedoms we easily take for granted. So I listen and learn, share and comment. And resist. I didn't realize it but I am pursuing the doctorate of my life in listening. Join me.

---

10   https://www.merriam-webster.com/dictionary/edify

11   "Algorithms Are Making American Inequality Worse" by Jackie Snow, Jan. 26, 2018, *MIT Technology Review*

12   "Autocratic Legalism" by Kim Lane Scheppele, *University of Chicago Law Review*, Mar 2018, Vol. 85 Issue 2, p545-583. 39p.

CHAPTER VII

When My "Be Best" Means "Be Black"

Nov. 25, 2018

When I wake up itching to write, that means something. My blogging can feel like the steam escaping a pressure cooker – forceful and insistent. In the process, the contents of the pot are transformed. When I write this way there is a distinct before and after. I change and am changed.

Did you know I am Black? Once upon a time I tweeted that I don't generally tell people this, I let them figure it out. I say that as someone who has spent the majority of her school and professional life embedded in predominantly white institutions (PWIs) which is to say I have always been aware of difference. Of *my* difference. But at the same time, I have also developed numerous means and methods to negotiate the ways I demonstrate, downplay or highlight that particular difference. It's a skill. It's a necessity.

When I was a girl, I tagged along with my mother to various meetings of civic and community organizations. I was great at stuffing envelopes and placing stamps. The women (it was almost always only women) talked and I listened, relieved to be busy rather than bored. My mother was an activist but I could not register her that way when I was growing up. She engaged in and also led organizations that advocated for all forms of social justice, many of those connected in one way or another to the Lutheran Church. At the time, I could not see these things as I see them now. I could not see her as I see her now.

In my 50's I see my mother in myself more clearly than at any other time. It's ironic. It was when she was in her 50's that I was perhaps the most captive audience to her movements (in every sense of the word), aged 8 to 18.

I hardly remember her speaking directly about her Blackness or being Black in those very white Midwestern Lutheran spaces. But I remember how well loved she seemed, how warmly we were welcomed to the summer institutes in Valpraiso, Indiana. And I felt like I fit right in with all those justice-loving offspring of so many church families from Wisconsin, Ohio, Indiana, Michigan, and Iowa. I suppose that's where I got my workshop start. It's funny to me that I would tell you about my mother when I thought I wanted to talk about something else.

I've been struck in the last several days by Black folks writing about being Black in white spaces. This recent essay[13] by Mychal Denzel Smith in *Harper's* speaks about the dilemma of the Black public intellectual under the influence of the white gaze.

> The white audience does not seek out black public intellectuals to challenge their worldview; instead they are meant to serve as tour guides through a foreign experience that the white audience wishes to keep at a comfortable distance. White people desire a representative of the community who can provide them with a crash course.

---

13   "The Burden of The Black Public Intellectual", Mychal Denzel Smith, *Haper's Magazine*, Dec. 2018 *https://harpers.org/archive/2018/12/the-burden-of-the-black-public-intellectual/*

Although I make no claim to being a public intellectual, I am a Black woman who writes publicly and shares distinct opinions. I recently had an experience that was somehow an ironic twist on this whole conversation.

I am scheduled to offer a workshop of the National Association of Independent Schools People of Color Conference (#NAISPoCC) in Nashville this week. The title is "Be The Power And The Point – Why You Need To Present At Your Next Conference" and the goal is to encourage more educators of color at all stages of their careers to consider presenting at education conferences or join organizations to help plan them. It's a *work*shop because participants will be doing the work of examining their areas of expertise and developing an intention going forward. My role is that of facilitator. In order to prepare I offered a test run of the session at my school and shared an invitation only a day in advance.

My international school has very few faculty and staff of color. And my session is geared specifically to that demographic. Nevertheless I did my level best to deliver the session as intended and I had a remarkable turnout which included the Director, all three principals, the Director of Technology, IB Coordinator and three faculty members. Of those attending three identify as people of color. I was thrilled at the show of support and interest. I have never had that kind of attendance for past workshops. In the end, it was a good choice. I received some useful feedback and lots of praise. I counted it as a very big win.

There was a moment during the session, however, where a question came up about how the message would be different for an audience of color. On the spot, I struggled to generate a satisfactory response. I mentioned a bit about the dimensions of the conference itself and the emotional experience of, for once, being in the beautiful and varied majority. But I couldn't get to the crux of my purpose. When I read Smith's essay about Black intellectual labor under the white gaze, my frontal cortex was lighting up with all sorts of recognition. In a later conversation with my colleague I was able to articulate the differences more clearly explaining, for instance, that as a white male with role authority he is accustomed to being given the floor. This is not the case for me as a Black woman. People will not naturally defer to me or my supposed expertise in a racially and/or gender-mixed group. I think he got it but it also reminded me of how possible it is to go through the world white, male and clueless about the visible and invisible differences of experience that play out in our daily lives.

My ethical survival revolves on not begrudging my colleague his question. In respecting his curiosity while at the same time granting myself the possibility of offering incomplete and imperfect responses I rebuild my capacity to continue engaging. I am under no obligation to take on the role of 'race whisperer' in any context. Yet as a fellow human with a different experience and outlook I aim to listen in pursuit of insight. For both of us.

To resist all this 'race talk' would seem a comfortable antidote for me and those like me in similar contexts. The option to try to simply "blend in" is always there, as unrealistic and impossible as ever. Deciding that my version of "Be Best" means "Be Black" and vocal and unapologetic is a renewable after-effect of writing publicly. My journey has been a long and highly circuitous one. I did not follow my mother's path immediately or fervently. All my recent 'race talk' is a late-stage development at best. My readings keep bringing me back to history which I at once resent and grudgingly accept.

Near the end of his generous book on how to have race conversations in the classroom [14], Science Leadership Academy educator, Matt Kay, tells us:

---

14   Kay, Matthew R., *Not Light, But Fire – How To Lead Meaningful Race Conversations In The Classroom*. Portsmouth, NH: Stenhouse Publishers. 2018.

Colonialism and antebellum slavery were buoyed by the most intractable ignorance; it took centuries of disruptive conversations to destabilize racism's most basic tenets. History remembers Douglass, but not the countless teachers, parents, and mentors, both enslaved and free, who kept the toughest conversations alive under the bleakest circumstances. These people had scant encouragement. They could more readily count on cynicism, apathy, or threats from power structures that benefited from their silence. (p. 261, *Not Light But Fire*, 2018)

Here we are and all of this sounds so familiar, so immediate, so *right now*. You and I belong to those countless teachers, parents, mentors who in 2018 and beyond must keep those very tough conversations alive and present. I have a platform. If I am not using it to bring others into the spotlight, to draw attention to disparities in experience, to grow our collective understanding of ways forward, then what am I doing?

CHAPTER VIII

Die *Sprachbürgerschaft* Explained

*Die Sprachbürgerschaft is a word
I made up in German. It translates to
"language citizenship" and it is the title
of a book of poems I published in 2016.*

February 2019

As an entry in the book[15], "*Die Sprachbürgerschaft*" is a fictional dialogue between a native German speaker and a foreigner (me) who speaks and writes German fluently. The native speaker's initial curiosity gradually gives way to skepticism, suspicion and finally resentment towards the foreigner who appears to be taking unwarranted liberties by daring to write and publish in a language she was not born into. "Language Citizenship"

---

15   Lyons-Halmer, Sherri. *Die Sprachbürgerschaft, Gedichte und anderes Zeug.* Hamburg: Tredition Verlag 2018.

connotes feeling at home in a second language without the full acceptance of the surrounding culture.

Both speakers in the dialogue treat language as a place. The native German speaker asks a range of questions like: "Did you grow up in this language? In which language were you born? How long have you been writing in this language?" When I reveal that I was born and raised in the American language, the native speaker registers surprise that I would choose to leave behind the language of "unlimited possibilities." The mood turns sour when the native speaker wonders if I actually hold "Language Citizenship". My obvious ignorance of the concept and its social necessity sends the native speaker into a low-key rage. How dare I write in a language for which I have no formal permission! Which then opens the door to a new wave of outrage describing the dangers of not maintaining language borders against foreigners who just show up and decide it's okay to speak and write in a language they were not born and raised in. I'm even accused of being a possible "'language anarchist or leader of a language cult." In closing the native speaker threatens to report me to the "language police."

Describing the dialogue in English feels both strange and freeing. While humorous, the fiction illuminates an underlying tension with being a visible immigrant in this tidy Alpine republic. "Language citizenship" is a thing I claim for myself because I know that it will never be conferred by my adopted culture no matter how long I stay or how assimilated I become. Language as a place creates a tangibility, a permanence that allows me to assert that the roots I have struck in this soil will outlast me.

My truth is this: I am an American immigrant. I immigrated to Austria in 1991. I retain my US citizenship although my permanent residence is in Vienna. In real terms, I am party to a number of privileges that flow from having a blue passport, being a native speaker of English, and working in an elite American institution. I am also a Black German-speaking woman in a country that specializes in hospitality. When I travel outside of Vienna, I am confident in my capacity to navigate a variety of social encounters. The country's economy depends on a long established reputation of welcoming tourists. Wherever I go, I look like a tourist.

At first glance in Austria I may not appear to belong. Then I speak. My language changes everything. By virtue of my skin color, people notice me. By showing a command of the language, I ensure that I will also be taken seriously. Speaking is my primary avenue for communicating in German. It's a means to an end; a tool for getting things done. At the same time, the German language remains a significant love of my life, a playground for a special kind of creativity.

To write myself into full authenticity, however, I choose English. I correspond with other English speakers, readers, writers. I stretch out lines of communication to educators across the globe via Twitter and my blog. German, on the other hand, is the language of traffic reports, hotel reservations, and radio listening. It's the language of my bureaucratic dissatisfaction and order-in menus. More often than not my German discourse seeks functionality and expediency; planning and follow through. German is my language of domesticity; in German I am settled. English then becomes my language of expansion and growth, of dreaming and collecting.

There is significance, too, in the fact that I was able to leave the land of "unlimited possibilities" yet never had to relinquish or silence my mother tongue. On the contrary, I moved to a country where my native language skills opened up numerous opportunities. My elevated immigrant status in Austria relies on the perception of English as a personal and professional asset. To be clear: by immigrating to Austria from the United States I have been able to build on my previous status markers of education and mobility. I live like a Black woman who is free: a Black woman who is free to think her thoughts, speak her mind and engage with others as an equal.

When I read and write about my country of origin from this distance I am exercising my privilege. Writing and reading at a distance means that I have breathing space to be critical, curious and observant. The distance affords me an independence that is distinct and fortifying. By living in Austria while writing my Black American woman self into being, I am claiming an intellectual/cultural/literary room of my own in the world. It has taken me a surprisingly long time to understand that the world typically does not give such rooms to Black women and girls. I've learned to create my own room right where I am.

"Language citizenship" is an imaginary thing, yes, and a surprisingly real means of claiming this life I've made in a country that, although I call it home, has no other way to categorize me than as a foreigner. Similar to being that rare Black person among large groups of white people, in Austria I am accustomed to being the acceptable exception. If language is a place, I have at least learned how to make myself at home. The world needs more free Black women. My words want to build spaces that welcome and foster free Black women and people who support them. Geography, in my case, poses a chance rather than a barrier to doing that.

CHAPTER IX

What Happened When I Went To School With My Hair Out

April 19, 2019

Hair out. That's how I'd have to say it, right?

Hair out, as in: not down, not "open" as one would say in German.

I wore my hair
my natural Black hair
out
at school
all day long.
Which is to say I wore an Afro.
An unpicked, unshaped tussle of curly strands
crowning my head.
A supersoft bouncy castle up top
framing my brown round face.

I added big dark sunglasses
and silver hoops,
Wore all black and a serious look
and suddenly my kids could not recognize
the teacher they were expecting.
Colleagues stopped in their tracks, smiled wide
then threw their roses at my feet.
Behind my glasses I felt protected, shielded,
safely distanced.
I kind of liked it.
My hair out
with its own righteous agenda
let me tap into
who I might be
if I chose
Not to give a damn
about packaging and expectations.
With my crinkly crown out and about
I cannot go unnoticed.
I cannot float under the radar.
I cannot not be seen.
Being able to choose visibility
and which damn to give
are privileges of the few.
But for a limited time only
I tested the waters and dabbled in a role
I could find becoming
and welcome:
sharp, fierce, unbothered;
proud Black all-woman.
Imagine what it means,
what it meant
to wear my hair out,
my eyes covered,

my expression nonplussed,
brown skin gleaming
surrounded by a well meaning white gaze
that wonders but can
never really know
the extent of that Black abundance.

Writing

CHAPTER X

Introduction

Part of my process involves explaining to myself why I am here and not there. Why I decided on this but not that. My reasons for writing have evolved over time. My reasons keep changing, the more I write.

These two pieces are attempts at understanding what I get when I give myself the space and time to put my thoughts in print.

CHAPTER XI

Author, Audience and Parts of Speech

Nov 1, 2015

For much of October, I have been mentally wringing my hands over exactly how I want to contribute to Digital Writing Month, especially as a featured contributor. I gladly accepted the invitation to be a part and was flattered to be included among a fascinating cross-section of participating authors. I kept asking myself—what do I have to share? What's my angle? What's important to me? What matters? And going a level deeper—what's at stake?

Let me start here. I write regularly in public online spaces. I blog, I tweet, I comment. In fact, if I google my name, I get four pages' worth of results which refer almost exclusively to one of those acts. So foremost in the digital warehouse of frequently accessed data points related to my name, writing pops up as if it were all that I do. So if Google's main clues suggest "Sherri Spelic writes," then that must make it so, right? Hmmm...

I realized only very recently that I want to talk about audience here. Because when I write, even when I say I don't think much about who is going to read whatever I put out there, of course that's a lie. I often consider for whom my words are intended. I care about reaching certain individuals and groups with my message. This thinking shapes, too, where I choose to publish—on my own blog or on a public platform like Medium.

Digital writing—in my understanding, the act of creating texts or other products through digital tools which are designed to be shared with readers via digital means—diverges significantly from the private hand-written journaling I did for years. From my laptop and occasionally from my tablet I draft texts which I primarily publish immediately. And when I say publish it means that I post it on my blog which triggers a least two separate tweets and sends out about 100 e-mails to subscribers of my blog. If I choose to publish on Medium I can either submit it for review to the editors of a specific publication or I can post it independently. In both cases, these texts are out there for anyone and everyone with reasonably free internet access to see, read, and also ignore.

But here's the thing: that "out there" business can be misleading. Just because anyone could find my beautifully crafted reflection on 'the joy of whatever' does not mean that many, or necessarily anyone will. We kind of assume that because the user base of the internet is so vast, diverse and active, that we who brave the waters of such relentlessly fast-paced media will be showered with attention from all angles, positive and negative. When we write our provocatively snarky think-piece on 'the rise and fall of you-know-what-I'm-talking-about', we can be so convinced that the masses will jump up, click and re-click their immediate approval and even the trolls will come marching into our comment stream to illustrate the vital nerve that we have touched. That, however, is so rarely how this digital writing thing actually unfolds, at least in my corner of the internet.

Here's where I think we can fall into a trap. We want audience. We want readers. We'd like to win over subscribers. We want to feel useful and appreciated and worthy and maybe even important. And audience seems like a way to get there. How many subscribers to your blog before you can call your writing endeavor a success? What's the critical mass of Twitter followers required to be considered a "thought leader"? How do you get to be listed as a LinkedIn Influencer when you post an article?

Because in digital media we like to let numbers and metrics tell the story—the story of reach, of clicks, of views, visits, and referrals. These metrics are then readily folded into narratives about popularity, trends, importance, because in the economy of attention, these things matter. These metrics tell us many things but they fail to tell us as writers and as people enough of what we really need to know: Whom did I reach? What was it that resonated? Where was I misconstrued? Then, going a little deeper: What is in this piece for me? What lessons do I want to keep for myself? What would I do well to let go of right now?

The information that we most often crave about audience typically reaches us through other avenues, if at all: via comments, tweets and retweets, shares across different platforms. And so much of all that will remain unknown. In digital writing, as in other forms of expression, we need to be okay with that.

So how do we find audience, after all?

If we want audience, then we must first and foremost *be* audience. We need to read widely and astutely. We need to pause as we read the work of others—and become permeable. Being an audience means letting others into our worlds, leaving space for the sparring and dancing of ideas. Being an audience means listening—dropping defenses, setting aside our emotional reactivity for a moment. When we do these things, we become an audience of value and increase the likelihood of helpful and constructive interaction. We acknowledge a response within and perhaps also 'out there', privately or publicly.

If we want audience, then we must first and foremost *be* audience. We need to read widely and astutely. We need to pause as we read the work of others—and become permeable.

For me, this slow and steady acculturation of *being* audience while growing audience has afforded me the opportunity to mature into this writing practice at my own pace. In fact when I examine the bulk of my digital work, I quite simply would characterize it as "writing back." So much of what I write emerges as necessary and somehow urgent responses—to something I read, saw, experienced, heard. I write back to authors. I write back to my students. I write back to my professional/personal learning network (PLN). I also write back to myself.

When I'm not writing I do many other things: I teach, I coach, I parent, I facilitate, I move, I read, I lead, I follow. And by now these aspects flow freely into my writing. The immediacy of the digital—the risk and opportunity of exposure coupled with the potential speed of engagement and response—for me, this underscores the imperative of *being the audience I want to have.* Remaining focused on the distinctly human dimensions of our lightning fast communication channels stands at the core of what, why and how I choose to create.

It may seem that we are all born under the sign of algorithms' ascendency and that the astrology of our common future may be reduced to a handful of branded provider platforms. Yet it is and will continue to be our choice to uphold and broaden the reach, impact, and benefit of the irreplaceably human in each of us whether we are reading, writing, listening, or speaking. We need to think about our offer as *both/and* rather than *either/ or*. Writer and listener. Reader and speaker. Being the audience that makes positive waves requires more from us as writers, educators, activists, and contributors and also serves to regularly remind us of what we are in fact here for.

What matters to me in contributing to digital writing month? Supporting audience in all its forms and iterations; making *audience* a 30-day verb.

CHAPTER XII

Blogging Beyond the Classroom – A Talk

December 9, 2016

Below is the text of the talk I gave at the panel discussion session at the National Association of Independent Schools People of Color Conference 2016. I shared the panel with Marcy Webb (@teachermrw) in person and Christopher Rogers (@justmaybechris), who was not able to join us on site. The full title of our session was "Blogging Beyond the Classroom: Online Engagement for Professional and Personal Growth."

While planning this short talk, I started out with all kinds of "what" – What I do and where and for whom on which platforms.

It took me some time and a dry run to realize that that is not what I really want to talk about. Rather I want and need to consider the "whys" of my writing, of my online engagement, of being here.

So while I have prepared these remarks for you, they are also words I need to hear myself speak in order to test their truth.

Some truths – here goes.

There are days when I cannot wait to be able to sit down at my laptop and write, write, write.

The more I write, the greater my appreciation for those who write better than I, the larger my confidence that I can become a better, stronger writer.

I write to understand.

When I tweet I join in conversations. When I blog I join in conversation.

I find community in conversation.

What I write about is deeply connected to what I read.

The fact that I am here to talk about something that I choose and love to do blows my mind.

Having a blog means having a space for me to place thoughts and ideas. My blog is a sense-making tool.

Publishing blog posts lets me invite others into my thinking and writing space.

Just because I offer an invitation does not mean that people will come.

By publishing publicly I do not get to choose whom I invite and who shows up.

When I read the work of others and comment thoughtfully, I join a conversation and add value.

My greatest insight so far, "If we want to have audience, then we must first and foremost be audience."

This is my motivation throughout my reading and writing cycles. Reading deeply, widely, consistently leads me to write as a response, as a means of processing. And as my own writing elicits response from others, I listen and think alongside others and we start a new cycle of reading to write, and writing to read.

In other words, my writing – tweeting, blogging, curating, publishing – are forms of call and response, call and response.

In other words, my writing
– tweeting, blogging, curating,
publishing – are forms of call and
response, call and response. I
do believe that you can write
your way out of ignorance.

I do believe that you can write your way out of ignorance.

When I started my blog, when I began tweeting, I was not aware of these things. I simply began and slowly found my way.

And I've had help and support. I have a "digital Godmother" who is Rafranz Davis, an outspoken tech integrationist out of Texas who welcomed me into edu-twitter like no other and made me feel at home. I found men and women in various education circles, both K-12 and post-secondary education who gladly supported my work, and welcomed my commentary. This has made me want to stay and build and most recently, learn how to resist the ravages of the current political climate.

I didn't realize the strength or depth of my political views until I began writing publicly.

I did not understand that being in contact and in dialogue with authors whom I admired would matter in the way that it does, both for me and them.

It took some time to appreciate that my voice, my style, my sense of urgency mattered to more than a few people.

Now I can begin to understand that when I write, I am being politically active. I am being culturally active. I am being educationally active. And over time, I walk that arc from being active to becoming an activist.

As I stand before you today I believe that I am in the midst of that process without having landed: Active on the way to becoming an activist.

No piece of my writing is fully done when it is published and finds an audience. It is always imperfect – my best shot at that moment- and I own that.

Once upon a time in grad school, I developed some theories of action for my practice as an education leader. At the top of the list was this: Care must be at the core of everything we do. At the time, although I was thinking about schools and the education communities we build and inhabit, I see now that this particular theory of action underscores all of my public work as a writer, contributor and digital interloper. I show up and speak up because I care. I enter into dialogue and cultivate relationships of support and encouragement to both demon-strate and receive care.

I am proud to be here in this space with all of you and can honestly say that my presence at this conference, on this panel, in this community is about care – our collective and individual care.

I hope that it is helpful.

Emotional Interlude

CHAPTER XIII

Emotional Interlude

Some stories insist that they be told.

This single blog post is one such story. I hadn't planned to include it in this selection, only refer to it in places. And then, upon rereading, I was struck by its emotional impact then and now. In hindsight I can recognize Audrey Watters' ideas as essential and transformative for me.

CHAPTER XIV

A Programmable Future

November 8, 2014

I experienced a rare moment this week. I read a post and quite simply it changed me.

The post helped me see what I was not seeing.

To recognize what I have been avoiding.

To be brave when my fear is the only audible voice I can hear.

The post I read was "The Future of Education: Programmed or Programmable" [16] by Audrey Watters. It is in fact the transcript of a talk she recently gave at Pepperdine University. I encourage you to read the full text to appreciate the strength and wisdom of her arguments.

The first point that got under my skin was this:

> Whether it's in a textbook or in a video-taped lecture, it's long been the content that matters most in school. The content is central. It's what you go to school to be exposed to. Content. The student must study it,

---

16 Audrey Watters, "The Future of Education: Programmed or Programmable " on Hackeducation.com, Nov. 4, 2014 http://hackeducation.com/2014/11/04/ programmed-instruction-versus-the-programmable-web

comprehend it, and demonstrate that in turn for the teacher. That is what we expect an education to do, to be: the acquisition of content which becomes transmogrified into knowledge...

...despite all the potential to do things differently with computers and with the Internet and with ubiquitous digital information, school still puts content in the center. Content, once delivered by or mediated through a teacher or a textbook, now is delivered via various computer technologies.

YES! Content is always at the center, of course. And what have I been working so hard to cultivate in the learning episodes that I design for others? Experience. I want my clients, participants, students, athletes to experience something, to feel something and thereby come to know "the thing" and what it may mean for them. Content has been a vehicle but my real desire has always been to generate feelings, emotions, connection – the stuff that makes you feel alive. How very counter-cultural I now understand.

Audrey Watters goes on to talk about shifting away from the content-centered approach of the "programmed web" and towards the more open and co-constructed "programmable web:"

The readable, writable, programmable Web is so significant because, in part, it allows us to break from programmed instruction. That is, we needn't all simply be on the receiving end of some computer-mediated instruction, some teacher-engineering. We can construct and create and connect for ourselves. And that means that—ideally—we can move beyond the technologies that deliver content more efficiently, more widely. It means too we can rethink "content" and "information" and "knowledge"—what it means to deliver or consume those things, alongside what it makes to build and control those things.

This is about where things started to heat up for me. The next sentence laid my purpose out for me like the Tarot card you knew was coming before you even approached the table:

> One of the most powerful things that you can do on the Web is to be a node in a network of learners, and to do so most fully and radically, I dare say, you must own your own domain.

WHAT?

As I read on, two things were happening: my emotions had gotten hold of the stage and were running with it. At the same time, my rational mind tore further into the text looking for something to save me fast.

> Authority, expertise, participation, voice—these can be so different on the programmable web; not so with programmed instruction. The Domain of One's Own initiative at University of Mary Washington purpose-fully invokes Virginia Woolf's A Room of One's Own: "A woman must have money, and a room of her own, if she is to write fiction." That is, one needs a space—a safe space that one controls—in order to be intellectu-ally productive.

Boom!

> We have an amazing opportunity here. We need to rec-ognize and reconcile that, for starters, in the content that programmed instruction—as with all instruc-tion—delivers, there is a hidden curriculum nestled in there as well. Education—formal institutions of schooling—are very much about **power, prestige, and control**. [emphasis mine]

And then this:

> Despite all the talk about "leveling the playing field"
> and disrupting old, powerful institutions, the Web rep-
> licates many pre-existing inequalities; it exacerbates
> others; it creates new ones. I think we have to work
> much harder to make the Web live up to the rhetoric
> of freedom and equality. That's a political effort, not
> simply a technological one.

That's when the tears came rolling in. Between the deep
desire to be that "node in a network of learners" and the self-
unhelpful stance of "I could never do that." (in this case to
have, run and maintain my own domain.), a larger truth was
revealed: I am at liberty to make use of my own superpowers.
I am a learner of outrageous potential. There is no reason to
believe that I cannot do what no one expects. That's when all
the forces, internal and external, technological and philosophical which have kept the volume of my fears turned all the way
up seemed suddenly muted.

I am at liberty to make use of my own superpowers. I am a learner of outrageous potential. There is no reason to believe that I can-not do what no one expects.

I've been sitting with this experience for a few days now. I
wrote to Audrey almost immediately to say Thank you and at
the same time nearly wanting to ask for the antidote. Because
it is a fundamentally scary experience to be exposed to your

own potential and grant it some credibility. And when you belong to a marginalized group, that exposure can be all the more astounding and confounding. Empowerment can feel like work because it is not for free. Empowerment always challenges us to imagine, to create, to put into practice what once appeared impossible.

Sharing

CHAPTER XV

Choosing Social Media

January 2019

My use of social media is a choice. I choose what to communicate across different platforms. I run risks of various shapes and sizes, none of which I imagine to be life or career threatening. But my imagination in this arena, I'll admit, is limited. Despite the digital company I keep, I do not doubt that I remain woefully naive about the potential damage I could possibly experience as a result of my exposure through the internet and all sorts of related services.

And yet here I am, here we are: connected and atomized, immersed and drowning, following and followed. In the early 2000's I could not have foreseen this development. I shunned mobile phones until I was given one as a gift in 2005 and only decided to purchase a smartphone in 2016. I never wanted to become as acclimated and attached to screen time as I am now. While I could tell you the story of my steady movement deeper and deeper into a very particular digital twilight zone, I'll spare you the details and offer you some essays that are like signposts along the way.

A few things are clear: I do Twitter. I rent a blog space from Wordpress. I maintain publication real estate on Medium. Occasionally I have been known to share a few words on Voxer in dedicated groups. Other than that, there's not much to boast. I deleted Facebook in 2018 but was never a heavy or even moderate user of the platform. I keep a profile up on Linked In but it is visibly outdated and less than personally relevant. That said, those are the moving pieces that I know about and actively attempt to moderate. Again, it would be ridiculously naive to believe that that's all there is. I have bread crumbs all over the internet and although technically not social media platforms, Google basically knows all my business and so does Amazon.

When I have chosen to write about social media a couple of things are typically going on: 1. I am trying to document my personal astonishment at the depths of my entanglements and 2. I am trying to get a grip on the breathtaking systemic implications of our reliance on digital services, literally from the cradle to the grave. I have no advice to give because I question the wisdom of my digital decision-making at every stage. What I have are my very particular and pedestrian experiences, primarily with a single platform as you'll see. There's a lot of wondering in these essays, less knowing.

I think I'm glad about that. Wondering is often more interesting than flat out knowing.

CHAPTER XVI

The Disconnect Amid So Much Connection

October 8, 2013

Just recently I willingly labeled myself a "lurker" [17] in order to describe my social media engagement as an educator. A lurker is someone who reads, follows, observes online conversations and postings *and* chooses not to publicly engage by producing output. I adopted the term because I felt that it best captured my own approach to this (for me) relatively new realm of professional and personal learning.

Here's the thing: As I read more and more posts concerning how to get more educators connected, the best way to initiate the uninitiated and essentially how to get more folks to jump on said bandwagon, I'm getting a little frustrated. I think it's the labeling we are using to frame the dialogue: connected vs. unconnected or semi-connected, initiated vs. uninitiated. After reading these terms I have essentially asked myself: What's the price of admission? At what level of output do I get to call myself "connected"? How many tweets until I become "a really

---

17 https://edifiedlistener.wordpress.com/2013/10/05/lurking-listening-and-proud-of-it/

useful educator"? It seems to me that the purpose embedded in so many labels serves to determine exactly this. If I make enough of my learning public through particular online forums (of which there are many, many), then I get to officially board the bandwagon and become its latest new ambassador.

As educators our most significant connection is, and remains, to our students. We connect through the care, concern, and respect we show each of our students every day.

While thinking (and getting all worked up) about this topic, I realized how much I long for a different tack in the conversation. As educators our most significant connection is, and remains, to our students. We connect through the care, concern, and respect we show each of our students every day. We connect when we reach out to parents and communicate our hopes, expectations, and desire for partnership in developing our young people. We connect in the way we share and collaborate with our colleagues across the hall, upstairs, in the next grade level, or even on the other side of town. We connect with our craft whenever we experiment with new ideas, take risks in our approaches and recognize our weak points. When we co-opt a term as broad as "connected" to define a fairly narrow range of activities and behaviors, we do ourselves and our colleagues a disservice. We create the "us and them" divide before we even can begin the conversation.

Edublogger, Tom Whitby argues in his latest post[18] that

> "Connected educators may be the worst advocates for getting other educators to connect. Too often they are so enthusiastic at how, as well as how much they are learning through being connected, that they tend to overwhelm the uninitiated, inexperienced, and un-connected educator with a deluge of information that both intimidates and literally scares them to death."

He may well be right. I appreciate his recognition that educators new to social media may be hard-pressed to comprehend the fervor of some, yet I can't help but chafe at the insinuation (in this post and others) that the "unconnected" among us represent so much lack in our whole education system. That may not be the intent yet I feel that sentiment come through again and again.

Come on, educators! We can do better than this! We can be enthusiastic about our turbo learning and wear our merit badges of connection and still remember that every time we divide ourselves, we lose more than we gain. Our "unconnected" colleague down the hall is still, first and foremost, our colleague with whom we share kids and a school community. We need to always be in the business of supporting each other in striving to serve kids and doing our best with what we have. Let's stay connected and let's address the core of the topic: how do we help each other achieve our professional best? Whether in person, on the phone, by e-mail, or online, let our connection, above all, be human, compassionate and genuine.

---

18   http://tomwhitby.wordpress.com/2013/10/07/patience-for-the-uncon-nected/

CHAPTER XVII

On the Other Side
of a Twitter Tizzy

March 30, 2015

One weekend I found myself in a Twitter tizzy. There was a chat conversation circling around the topic of how the term "connected educator" is defined. One camp insisted that it must involve the use of social media while the other camp argued that being connected may include other forms of communication, not exclusively social media. You can read the bulk of that conversation here [19].

My immediate reaction was annoyance and frustration, then anger. I definitely identify with the "let's be more inclusive and drop the exclusionary language" camp and have written as much before. But what got under my skin on this occasion had to do with my perception of who fell into which camps. Older white males whose prominence in edu social media appears to hinge on maintaining very strict definitions as to who may call themselves an equally "connected educator" were clearly arguing their cause. While in the other camp, there were white women and a few white males claiming that the insistence

19   https://twitter.com/jleung10/status/582178812911288320

on the use of social media actively diminishes other forms of connection which educators may employ to improve their practice and reach out to colleagues in the field. As far as I could observe there were no participants of color in this particular thread of conversation.

Of course, my perception of the situation has everything to do with the filters I applied: race, gender, relative social media rank among convo participants. As an African-American woman educator who is very active on at least one social media platform, I took objection to what I observed as typical brandishing and assertion of white male privilege to make and affirm the rules of belonging based on their relative standing in the social media edusphere (i.e., 35-55k followers on Twitter). This made me angry. And I don't enjoy being angry.

So I reached out to a couple of my social media mentors asking them to help me put my anger in perspective. Both were helpful. Rafranz Davis wrote back:

"Don't ever be afraid to disagree. That's where great ideas are born."

So I added my 2 cents, sharing a post I wrote 2 years ago on the same topic [20] and moved on. Before going to bed last night, however, I took another moment to reflect in my journal on what had gone on inside me, above all.

As I began to break it down for myself I also could see that beyond the righteous indignation about turf claiming on social media, I had my own little ego show going on. A further part of my frustration through the course of my reaction to this conversation had to do with not feeling adequately recognized, as if I had said nothing at all. My ego was bruised. And there's the kicker: I was in some ways guilty of the very same motives I was negatively assigning to others. I wanted to gain the

---

20 https://edifiedlistener.wordpress.com/2013/10/08/the-disconnect-amid-so-much-connection/

attention I believed I deserved and since that wasn't happening I was also beginning to stew.

This is such an interesting aspect now that I've put it out there. My righteous indignation over the turf wars remains and I stick to it. At the same time, I realize that in a public forum such as Twitter, other factors may also be at play, whether we are aware of it or not. I feel grateful for the lesson here. Seeing how vulnerable my ego is in this environment is absolutely instructive and provides me insight for appreciating more fully where others may be coming from especially when they are worked up about a topic. Even my "side" of the story turns out to be multifaceted. My challenge going forward will be in allowing others to live and express their multifaceted identities and ideas particularly when they do not align with my own.

Never The Same Twitter

June 27, 2016

I am currently in Denver attending the International Society for Technology in Education (ISTE) Conference. As the title suggests, this space focuses on teaching and learning with the support of educational technology, or ed tech. Attendees may be teachers, technology specialists, industry representatives, school district administrators and staff, school administrators, education media folks and certainly many others who may not fit into any of those boxes. The point is that there are over 16,000 people assembled here to delve into all things ed tech and related.

I happen to be here by a series of connections and events fueled by my engagement on Twitter. As @edifiedlistener, I have built up significant friendships and collegial bonds which have allowed me to broaden my perspective as an educator, writer, and citizen. To find myself in this hotbed of ed tech enthusiasm and celebration, though, comes as a bit of a surprise. While I am a ready learner of new tools and applications, I am conservative in the use of tech in my classroom which happens to be the gym

(I'm a physical education specialist). Although loyal to Twitter, I make only very limited use of other social media platforms. And especially noticeable in this specific environment, I do not yet own a smartphone. (An iPad, yes but no smartphone).

This may seem a minor thing. I assure you, in this environment, it is not. As mobile technology has shaped the current wave of tech innovations, the focus on smartphones for the delivery of all manner of services is unmistakable. Messaging in various forms, location services, on-the-spot information retrieval—these are some of the most urgent needs being met via smartphones on a minute to minute basis. Onsite it means that many activities and demonstrations rely on the assumption that participants bring this essential tool to the table (like having a pen and paper in previous iterations). While I can do plenty with my iPad and do not miss having a second device in my hands at the moment, there is a difference that is worth noting.

The observation has also led me to wonder about what other sorts of divides exist for students, educators, and citizens when an essential tool (on which heaps of services and uses are predicated) is absent. When we're in this center of ed tech creativity and invention, it's easy to forget that our fundamental assumptions (like widespread and sufficient internet access) may be absolutely false in various contexts. How do we account for those circumstances and those populations? Questions which bring me to the idea behind the actual title of this post: Never The Same Twitter.

When we use Twitter or other social media platforms, or even Google search for that matter, we rarely explore the fact that what appears on our individual screens is a function of who we are in terms of what we have searched for in the past, whom we have chosen to follow, whom we have accepted as friends. For every single one of us as users, the results are always different, even if not immediately noticeable. That's the power (and the risk) of sophisticated algorithms in all of our devices and the software they run. On the one hand, that can be cool. I follow people who interest me on Twitter and therefore benefit from their insights, shares, and connections. At the same time, however, I build a significant filter bubble [21] which shields me from messages and input from people and events I do not follow or find interesting.

I was thinking about this as I scrolled through my Twitter feed last night. While there was a fair amount of #ISTE2016 and #NotAtISTE2016 to be found, even more dominant were reports and shares from the Black Entertainment Television Awards #BETAwards. Beyonce and Kendrick Lamar apparently pulled off another performance milestone to top previous showstoppers at the Grammy Awards and Super Bowl Halftime earlier in the year. But the real deal came later when Jesse Williams gave his Humanitarian Award acceptance speech [22].

For me, as an African American woman, mother, educator, and citizen, this speech made all the difference. It spoke to me on so many levels, also as a writer and speaker. The message and the art of the message converged to make this a towering media experience for me for which I could not (and refused to) contain my emotion. No surprise, it arrived through Twitter. Through my very unique and individualized Twitter, multiple times.

For most of my colleagues at this huge conference, I bet this was not the case. There is no judgment here, just observation. For others, news of the Chilean win at the Copa America [23] through a penalty shoot out against Argentina perhaps had priority. Or further news regarding fallout from the UK Brexit

21 Eli Pariser, *The Filter Bubble, What The Internet Is Hiding From You.* New York: Penguin. 2011.

22 http://fusion.net/story/316998/jesse-williams-bet-awards-speech/?utm_source=twitter&utm_medium=social&utm_campaign=socialshare&utm_content=theme_top_mobile

23 http://www.espnfc.us/report?gameId=444696

vote[24]. The possibilities and variations of interest are too massive to contemplate—which constitutes an ideal proposition for the use of powerful algorithms that sort, filter and deliver the interests we want. If nothing else, this example should give us pause in noticing how distinct our filter bubbles are and become over time.

I have used my platforms to share my enthusiasm about #ISTE2016 AND one of the best speeches on the state of Black America I have ever witnessed. I hold space for both and it feels vital that I communicate that aspect with all the energy at my disposal. Considering all of the promises that technology holds, it strikes me that the greatest hurdles to real progress are in fact our narrow minds which resist being "blown" by outside and unfamiliar perspectives. This is the tremendous task we educators, both at #ISTE2016 and #NotAtISTE2016, need to fiercely pursue: investigating and interrogating our own and each others' filter bubbles to facilitate our collective growth and maturity now and not in some distant future.

We have to remember that even when we see and hear each other on social media channels, no two experiences are entirely alike. The sooner we understand this and actively work with the diversity at our fingertips, the better our chances of creating a more just and humane environment for our children and ourselves.

---

24   http://www.bbc.com/news/uk-politics-32810887

CHAPTER XIX

Speaking Digital PD

February 7, 2017

I recently held a workshop entitled: "Navigating The Blogosphere and Social Media for Professional Growth." It's a long title for a few simple ideas. I designed this 90 minute session as an interactive, experience-sharing and question-growing learning event and that's mostly what it turned out to be, according to participant feedback. I'm glad about that.

While part of my aim was to encourage participants to seek out social media opportunities to grow their professional practice and connections, I found that there was more I wanted to say. So often in promoting digital tools in education spaces, we emphasize all the things we can get from them: lesson plans, snappy ideas, old wine in new bottles, new wine in virtual bottles and on and on. There is no doubt much to be had, to be consumed, to be added to our overflowing professional plates.

At the same time, there is a piece that is so often ignored or hardly mentioned: the potency of our contribution. Yes, bloggers will tell you to blog, and that others can benefit from your hearing your story. This is true and frequently shared. The missing piece, however lies not simply adding to the jumble of voices but to *take an active part in creating and sustaining community.*

That means finding ways to acknowledge the voices you respect, giving credit where it is due, providing feedback and links which may benefit others. I summed up this idea in the slide: "Go for what you crave, stay to make the space a richer one." Show up on social media and be an example of positive digital citizenship: be kind, be thoughtful, be you. Make social media spaces better by being a good human.

The other point I wanted to emphasize with regard to social media use is that only you know (and will find out) what (and how much) is good for you and your aims (recognizing, too, that this will shift and change over time). Resist the pressure to try all platforms or to be everywhere at once. Let those impulses die a quick death. Instead, find the things that you find useful, do those and skip the rest. If Pinterest works for you in your private life, it may be a tremendous resource for your classroom or office needs. On the other hand, if you feel especially comfortable with Facebook, why not seek out like-minded groups there to begin your journey into education conversations in the digital sphere? Start somewhere and go from there.

If our goal is to encourage and empower colleagues, students, parents, administrators and policy makers to engage in education conversations on various channels, we need to think about how we welcome them into spaces which are new to them but territory to us. In that process we also need to break open our ideas about what Professional Development is and can be. This is as true for us as it is for the systems we inhabit and sustain.

I don't consider myself a digital evangelist. I do consider myself an active member of the commons who appreciates and uses digital tools. This distinction matters to me. And that is what I aim to share with colleagues when I find myself speaking digital.

CHAPTER XX

Nobody's Version of Dumb

September 9, 2017

I spend a lot of time on Twitter. I follow more people than I can actually keep up with and miraculously a bunch more follow me and I apologize that I can't just follow right back. I'm overwhelmed. I lose threads and also get lost in reading. I miss a lot and what I catch can probably be attributed to Twitter's algorithmic sorting which keeps the folks I most interact with close to the top of the tweets I will see. It's an imperfect system. My interests and responses are being guided, steered, nudged to achieve the golden data outcome of 'maximum engagement.' As long as I keep clicking around on the platform and rewarding the algorithm that delivers those precious "In case you missed it" messages, I am holding up my end of the user-platform bargain. Twitter stays in business and I cultivate my little networked worlds almost as intricately as my 9 year-old's Minecraft creations.

Then along comes a short thread like this [25]:

> no surprise. I find my twitter network to be homogenous. Tweet something that resonates, RTs happen. Tweet something out of scope. Crickets — *George Siemens (@gsiemens) September 7, 2017*

> Social media is a net negative. It has closed us off and created little safe spaces where we talk with people we agree with.

> — George Siemens (@gsiemens) September 7, 2017

> Sadly, bright and intelligent people are reduced to RTing pithy statements rather than thinking. Twitter makes smart people dumb.

> — George Siemens (@gsiemens) September 7, 2017

There's more but that's the core.

I know this lamentation. It is familiar and well worn and different figures deploy it at different junctures. Of course, @gsiemens is not just anybody. He's a public intellectual, well recognized in the tech and higher ed circles I frequent. So I also hesitate to publicly push back on this particular take. But, alas. I get tired of authority type voices telling me and others that Twitter is making us dumb.

Speak for yourself, I say. Rain on your own parade, not mine.

Look. Not everyone who comes to social media is looking for a fight. We have not arrived here to recreate Greek forms of debate. We are not showing up so that we can rattle our intellectual sabres. We are not turning up to punch each others' academic lights out, argument for carefully crafted argument.

I, for one, came because I was looking for others who could help me grow. I was in the market for good writing and good people and I found them. The longer I stayed and the more I

---

25 https://t.co/SXl5NtSRcL

engaged, good people *found me*. Good writing – I mean, strong, critical, robust and also sensitive writing walked right up to me and said, "Hi!" I got involved. I created adjoining spaces and fashioned a new home to welcome some of that rich writing. And I found art, humor, compassion, support, care, and *praise hands* Black Twitter. My life has been tremendously enlivened and broadened through my social media connections.

I am a smart person who is more open, more aware, more vocal and more critical due to my connections via social media.

You will rarely find me putting up my verbal dukes on Twitter but I will support those who do it well. When status heavy voices trot out these blanket statements about our shared intellectual demise, they offer a point of view that can be as narrow and constrained as those they accuse of the same offense. And often such voices enjoy the comfort and yes, privilege, of established recognition through institutions, publications, speaking invitations and considerable social media reach. These statements seem to come when these, usually male, individuals no longer feel "challenged" – when their membership in the social media 'Gifted and Talented' program is losing clout.

When I first ran across this thread, I wanted to ignore it. Give it the 'ho, hum, somebody's bored' non-response. But the annoyance stayed with me because I felt in those few tweets that my experience and the experience of too many others were being denied. And thoughtlessly so.

Some of us are here for community; to gather and confer with the like minded. To remind each other that our presence matters. For someone with a particular kind of status, this aspect might easily be overlooked. Not for me. I come to Twitter to prove to myself again and again that I have a voice and know how to use it. In other circles, my voice, my presence runs the very real risk being inaudible, invisible. But for someone who is accorded a certain level of authority, this instance may not occur or even register.

Formulating this kind of push back takes energy. It takes energy away from some things I'd rather read and write about. And I don't wish to expend more energy delving into the right-left Twitter divide article which prompted these tweets. When George Siemens claims that his network is fairly homogeneous, that is something that he can fix if it's a priority. But to drag us all down into a space that he in a later tweet describes as "closed, intolerant, narrow minded, and short sighted" is decidedly unfair and unnecessary and I refuse to be placed there by proclamation from on high.

Maybe this is precisely how and why I persist on social media: Refusing to be placed somewhere by someone who is not me. I place and position myself. I speak my own mind. I pick my own battles. I am nobody's version of dumb.

* Not long after this post went edu-viral, George Siemens reached out to me via e-mail. We had a helpful exchange and reached a mutual understanding that has served us well to this day. It's important to share this aspect of the story that is far less sensational and attention-grabbing. We both grew as a result of engaging.

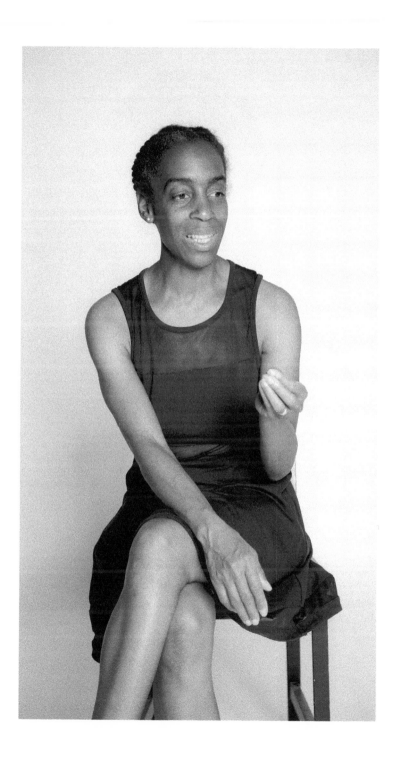

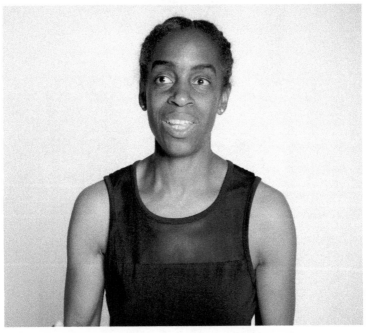

Interlude

CHAPTER XXI

Identity, Education and Power: Square One

Jan 29, 2016

Welcome to Identity, Education and Power. My name is Sherri Spelic and I am your host. This is Square One.

Square One traditionally refers to a place we return to after we've moved out, made some mistakes and need to start over. Most often we speak of "going back to square one." I want to re-purpose the term, however, for this auspicious occasion: the launch of a fresh new publication: **Identity, Education and Power.** And in this case, Square One is our excellent point of departure; the space from which this publication moves forward.

Square One is the singular true beginning, the unmistakable port of origin. And all origins have stories.

I've been writing for a long time now. My first piece of writing to receive public recognition was a contest essay I wrote in eighth grade. I belonged to a class of 10 in a small parochial school in one of Cleveland's working class communities. The contest essay was an assignment, not a choice. The topic was grandly formulated: *What America Means To Me.* I remember my classmates talking about their chosen themes—specific historical events or a general recounting of American history—and not being able to relate. I wrote differently, apparently. I took the prompt fully to heart and wrote a patriotic masterpiece which impressed the jury and earned me a $50 savings bond (in 1979 dollars).

Surprisingly, I still have that essay in my archives. Expertly laminated by my educator mother and preserved for eternity. It's a peculiarly interesting read almost 40 years later. According to my mother, the contest's sponsor representative who handed over the prize money at our school's awards banquet seemed a little taken aback when a skinny Black girl rose to claim the honor. I suppose that when the Ladies Auxiliary of the Polish Legion of American Veterans envisioned their contest, I, or anyone who looked like me, probably did not enter their imagination as the likely recipient of such an award. But it was essay #6 that won; not my face or outward features. It was my writing which earned me the recognition. That's important to remember.

Maybe that was when I first recognized the power of words. Of my own words. I discovered that I could win recognition, praise, accolades, ribbons and certificates (I especially liked ribbons and certificates) by using my words.

Fast forward to high school in the early 80's, when my writing received more training, fine tuning and acclaim. The crowning success? Admission to my first-choice Ivy League school. I attribute that outcome, at least in part, to my application essay. It was the one college essay that I enjoyed writing and was actually proud of. Asked to talk a bit about myself I ended up describing a shelf of various artifacts in my bedroom. The open-ended prompt allowed me to respond in a way that was what we would now call 'authentic.'

Decades have passed and I continue to write and write and write. In that time I have journaled, translated, commented, conceptualized, and more recently blogged. It's hard for me to imagine not writing something in some capacity. And now I've decided that it's time to expand my horizons; to employ my writing to support the other thing I love so dearly: reading.

While I deeply enjoy the rapid fire exchange of good, better and best reads to be found in my Twitter feed, I recently determined that I wanted something different. Something specific, something I hadn't quite found yet in my online travels: a space dedicated to Identity, Education and Power.

When I first checked on Medium this is what I got:

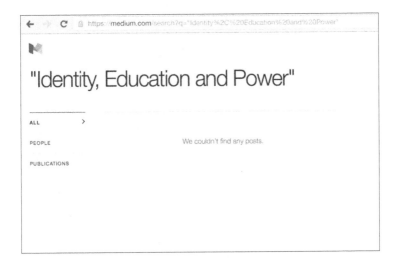

Imagine that.

I chose Identity, Education and Power because I realized that experiencing, and connecting these 'Big Three' are what I do, all day, every day. These are where my work is housed and rooted. They are my fields of struggle and triumph. Identity, Education and Power are *what* I write as much as *why* I write. But here's the thing: *I* is not enough. Even in the multiple aspects and levels of identity which I present—this alone is not enough. My online handle is @edifiedlistener. I am edified by and through listening.

I become more of who I am and wish to become by listening. **This publication is a public space for the listening I wish for and savor: Ideas of substance and heart; voices bearing strong words, soft words, thoughtful and bold words. Above all, this is a listening space.**

In the concept building phase of this publication I was reminded of a text I encountered a year or two ago on the subject of curating. Written by Hans Ulrich Obrist, curator of Serpentine Gallery London at the time, this short meditation spoke to me on a surprisingly personal level:

> ... I believe to 'curate' finds ever wider application because of a feature of modern life impossible to ignore: the incredible proliferation of ideas, information, images, disciplinary knowledge, and material products we all witness today. Such proliferation makes the activities of filtering, enabling, synthesizing, framing, and remembering more and more important as basic navigational tools for twenty-first century life. These are the tasks of the curator, who is no longer understood simply as the person who fills a space with objects but also as the person who brings different cultural spheres into contact , invents new display features, and makes junctions that allow unexpected encounters and results. [26]

"The person who brings different cultural spheres into contact..." That's me—or at least whom I aspire to be. The inauguration of this publication is my start button. Another nudge came to me through one of my edu-heroes, Audrey Watters, almost a year ago. At the time I was completely bowled over by the way her words spoke to and inspired me. When I wrote about

26 "To Curate" in *This Will Make You Smarter*, John Brockman, Ed., London: Transworld Publishers. 2012. pp. 118–119

it, I was coming to terms with stepping into my own power. [27]
What Audrey did for me with a single piece of writing was name
both my fear and my desire:

> One of the most powerful things that you can do on
> the Web **is to be a node in a network of learners,** and
> to do so most fully and radically, I dare say, you must
> own your own domain. (Emphasis mine. See essay
> "A Programmable Future" on pg. 75 for more thoughts
> on the subject.)

"To be a node in a network of learners.." That's me now, doing this. The publication **Identity, Education and Power** is one
such node—*of my creation.* I didn't ask anyone for permission.
I simply decided to start. Although this publication is technically not a domain, it is *my* domain. A space for which I am the
gatekeeper and host.

The first authors you will meet here have been invited to contribute. I have gone knocking on their digital doors, requesting
their involvement and in many cases, asking them to "Please
say yes." Overlap and intermingling between contributors and
readers is precisely my aim. You are all my guests and it is my
pleasure to welcome you into this newly christened space. It's
time to leave Square One.

Let the adventure begin!

---

27   See essay "A Programmable Future", pg. 73

Thinking About Education

CHAPTER XXII

Expanding the Narrative: Observing Eucation

My workspace at home which is one end of a dining table (that we rarely use for dining) stays cluttered with papers and books. Most of these are my own things with a little overlap from my youngest son's homework pages. Currently one book is on top of the pile next to my laptop and I've just peeked into the introduction. In *We Got This* [28], Language Arts educator and popular speaker, Cornelius Minor, tells me some things I both want and need to hear. He advocates strongly for listening to students and disposing of teacher hero narratives in the singular. In describing those people who would stand in the way of achieving equitable outcomes for all students, he suggests that the singular hero narratives perpetuate unrealistic expectations of individual teachers. Among those pernicious

---

28   Minor, Cornelius. *We Got This: Equity Access and the Quest to Be Who Our Students need Us to Be.* Portsmouth, NH: Heinemann, 2019.

ideals he lists relentless sacrifice, false sainthood, and mystic capabilities. As a corrective, this sentence stands out for me:

> "One way to take your voice back is to expand the narrative." p. 6

In the course of my blogging journey, I have written about many things but few themes surface as persistently as questions about education. What it is, how it works and for whom, under which conditions. To question education, to interrogate its premise means questioning society and its premises. A pebble of inquiry into schools as systems creates ripples of concern that extend to governance and funding structures, staffing choices, community resources, socioeconomic levels, partisan interests, and of course, the needs of students bound up in these contexts. None of these elements present stand-alone factors. My inquiries have consistently shown me that the webs of influences are both dense and unique to the particular setting. Every time I learn a little bit over here, I become starkly cognizant of all the factors I am missing in order to comprehend the conditions in a different space. I write about education as a means to learn.

As a parent, teacher and student it has taken time, energy and a bit of stubbornness not to mistake schooling for education. Yes, they are intimately related but it is vitally important to understand that one can be and become educated outside of formal school settings. It's possible to achieve remarkable expertise in a given area outside of designated training environments. Humans are built to learn through a variety of means both passive and active, by observing and doing, by visualizing and imitating, by teaching and being taught, in schools and beyond schools. I have spent far more years of my life in schools than elsewhere and I appreciate the importance they can have in the lives of people from all kinds of backgrounds. At the same time, it behooves me, as a "school veteran" to also consider what school may not be good for, where it falls short, and under which circumstances it emerges as a barrier rather than a vehicle.

As someone who writes about teaching and therefore about education, finding my voice has meant expanding my own narrative and understanding of what education is and does. The more I have written, the wider I have cast my net of observation and I have applied more varied lenses. Whether reading about classrooms or professional conferences, I have learned to look for clues about the role of social identities, of economic interests, political signaling—all of which reveal information about power dynamics. When we speak of narratives, we must also ask: who gets to shape and tell the story and insure that it reaches its intended audience? In every story about education, we must also train our eyes on the lines of power.

When I read Cornelius's words about taking my voice back, I heard the call to recover it from the dominant narratives. Stretching beyond the confines of my classroom, my institutions, my geographical context, I listen and respond to other writers who describe what ails and may also heal education. Here in these essays I have created a laboratory for questioning particular education narratives and gradually proposing some of my own, fresh narratives.

CHAPTER XXIII

Knee-Jerk vs. A Stone's Throw

April 9, 2015

I read that article. Yes, *that* article. You know the New York Times article [29] about Success Academy Charter Schools; about how they employ rigid and punitive teaching and management methods to produce very strong standardized test results. Yeah, that article. You read it too, right? And what was your response? Outrage? Indignation? Horror?

In my Twitter feed (which is how I was introduced to the article in the first place), I found an assortment of these reactions which, not surprisingly, resonated. No, I would not wish for my own children to experience that type of schooling. Yes, I find it deplorable that public shaming of underperforming students is relied on as a viable teaching and motivational strategy. Yes, I concur that the definition of academic success as evidenced by high test scores is narrow and misleading. And no, I do not believe for a moment that Ms. Moskowitz and her billionaire

---

29 'At Success Academy Charter Schools, High Scores and Polarizing Tactics" by Kate Taylor, April 6, 2015, *New York Times*.

backers care as much about the improvement of outcomes for poor brown and black children as they claim to.

After reading and re-reading the article, I found my desire and need to cast the Success Academy Charter Schools and their feckless CEO, Eva Moskowitz as the obvious villains nearly irresistible. Because we have a narrative here. And our brains are hard-wired for stories. The story goes: innocent poor brown and black children and their families become pawns in a much larger political and financial shell game in which obscenely wealthy hedge fund managers use education reform efforts as a cover for protecting their financial gains in the short and long term. (See this article for more [30].) Poor brown and black families in this narrative lack agency and wits to do much beyond make the most of the hands they are dealt. At the same time, middle class liberals protest on the street and via social media while sending their own children to imperfect yet workable public and private schools. This is what I perceive to be a widespread narrative. It is simplistic, has fairly flat characters and beyond the occasional ideological skirmish, offers little in the way of visible action.

The reality, however, is and must be so much more complicated, messy and multifaceted than this particular narrative. Each intersection of individuals – students, teachers, parents, principals, charter CEO – yields a host of perspectives and ideas which may blend, align, collide, or explode at various junctures. That's the picture that is so much harder to show. Because it's more than a picture; these are phenomena unfolding in real-time where not all elements are on display or available for armchair interpretation. While the flat narrative fits nicely with my pre-selected biases, my thinking, and worse, my potential understanding are weaker for taking this story at face

---

30 "Nine Billionaires Are About to Remake New York's Public Schools" by George Joseph. March 24th, 2015, *The Nation*. Republished on truth-out.org

value. If I step away from the flat narrative, then I must also acknowledge all the things about which I know next to nothing.

I do not teach and have never taught in a public school. Or in a charter school. I do not live in New York City nor have I ever. I am African-American and my upbringing was distinctly middle class. I have never lived in poverty and I cannot claim to know that experience. The list could go on and on. What I do have are beliefs about society, about education, about the power of writing, about the power of reading and dialoguing to further and deepen my understanding of the world you and I inhabit. I also have my unique life experiences which inform and also filter my perceptions of what *is* and what is *true*.

While I find the portrait of Success Academy Charter Schools and their model of academic progress depicted in this single article both troubling and frightening, I must also recognize that I am not that parent whose child is thriving in that environment. I am not that student who feels like this teacher cares about her more than all her previous teachers. I am not the young ambitious educator out to change the world who gets promoted to principal at 25. There are beneficiaries in every system. My point here is that in our eagerness to judge, judge, judge, we are deeply prone to dismissing the experiences of those whose achievements we might well applaud in other contexts which align more conveniently with our unique set of biases.

One of the questions that came up for me as I continued to turn these contrary thoughts in my head was: Could it be that this portrayal irks us so much because it reflects how we actually do school, just taken to an ugly extreme? Because looking at my own teacher behaviors: I line kids up and walk them from place to place, I shush them, I insist on quiet when I am or others are talking, I have shamed children, I have not allowed every child to use the toilet when he or she wanted. Again my list could go on. Many of the practices which offend our particular sensibilities that appear in the article may prove to be extreme versions of what many of us do already.

I came across a post by Chris Hedges calling for boycotts, divestment and sanctions [31] against corporations which feed off the prison economy. While the context of the remarks below refer to the blatant injustices of penal culture in the US, this passage strikes me as painfully applicable here:

> Michelle Alexander, the author of *The New Jim Crow*, is outspoken about the imperative for organizing to fight back. In a speech at Union Theological Seminary in New York City in March she told her audience [32]:

> "Jesus taught that he who is without sin should cast the first stone. Well, we have become a nation of stone throwers. And in this era of mass incarceration it is not enough to drop your stone. We have to be willing to catch the stones raining down on the most vulnerable. And we must be willing to stand up to the stone throwers and disarm them."

"We have become a nation of stone throwers."

This sentence hits home on so many levels. Whenever I deign to talk about what education should be, particularly for other people's children, then I need to check and see which stones I am carrying and prepared to cast. Which assumptions am I holding that may cloud my capacity to see what I wish was not there? How and to what degree am I perpetuating and further entrenching negative practices? Hard questions and very necessary questions. We cannot go on espousing the importance of critical thinking for our students, in our curricula, throughout

---

31 Boycott, Divest and Sanction Corporations That Feed on Prisons" By Chris Hedges. https://www.commondreams.org/views/2015/04/06/boycott-divest-and-sanction-corporations-feed-prisons

32 Found at https://www.youtube.com/watch?v=T79I1PLT5Ks&t=93s

our standards, if we are not willing and able to deconstruct the narratives we create and support in our own minds.

Stop and look at the stones you are holding.

Hat tip to my Twitter dialogue partners who really helped me arrive at a deeper level of reasoning on this topic:

@Sisyphus38

@JustinAion

@pepinosuave

@LubaSays

@NA_Dellsey Thanks, all!

CHAPTER XXIV

There Is No App for Patience

June 30, 2015

There is no app for patience. Just as there is no app for respect, kindness or trust. I say this now in the midst of all the hoopla around the International Society for Technology in Education (ISTE) conference currently taking place in Philadelphia not so much because I want to rain on anyone's edtech parade, but because I am missing something. So much of our focus on the use of technology in education has to do with speed, efficiency and scale – measurable features. We talk about technology as an accelerator of learning, we extol the virtues of tremendous reach when tens of thousands register to join a popular Massive Open Online Course (MOOC). We laud countless applications and software packages which promise us time-saving and economizing means to teach our classes and "raise achievement" in the process. I get it. There are numerous digital tools which allow us to do things we couldn't do before as easily such as locate, sort and store information. As individuals we can create media to share with a potential worldwide audience. And our societies are heading increasingly in the direction of more technology, of faster tools, of ubiquitous digitization of the billions of data points that make up our individual lives. I do not live under a rock. Nor do you.

There is no app for patience. Just as there is no app for respect, kindness or trust.

Still, there is no app for patience nor will there ever be.

Patience is a human capacity to do more than wait. Patience describes the capacity to pay close enough attention, to develop the awareness of self and others. Patience is the quality that enables us to recognize and evaluate when pausing, waiting, holding off will likely bring about a better, more robust and lasting outcome than not waiting in a given situation. Listening often requires patience. Cultivating anything that grows requires patience. Any learning process aimed at achieving depth demands patience. Not surprising then that patience would seem to be a prerequisite for any educational endeavor – whether teaching or learning. In our current discourse around education – be it policy, practice or vision – patience finds no mention, no foothold, carries no weight.

On the contrary, impatience is the working assumption. We simply cannot wait. We should not wait. And for many issues I would perhaps echo that sentiment. Impatience is warranted and called for in response to racialized police violence, in response to ending childhood poverty, in response to highly inequitable school systems. There are many areas where we as a society cannot wait to tackle certain issues. But when it comes to individual students and teachers and their progress, in their capacity to effect change, where is our patience and empathy? When it comes to policy makers setting standards for multiple school districts and expecting to see rapidly improved results within the 9-month sprint we call a school year, where do we find patience and common sense?

There is no app which will teach us or train our patience. Patience requires some depth of thought. Patience requires being able to slow down when the rest are speeding by in order to see precisely what is happening. Patience with our kids means daring to watch and wait before we rush in with an intervention. Patience with our teachers means trusting them to make decisions which benefit and grow student learning and not assuming that all the results of that learning will show up through standardized testing. Patience with our colleagues means listening and encouraging without shaming and judging. Patience creates space for individual variability. Patience provides a stepping stone for faith and positive belief. Patience allows us to spend time not knowing. Patience can teach us to listen first before we speak; to observe carefully before we evaluate.

Patience is something I miss in our education talk and behavior. We cannot copy and paste patience into our curricula or teaching practice. It will need to come from within us and our institutions. Creating space for patience in a school would require a seismic shift in culture and habits. Some schools enter through mindfulness practice. I hope more will choose to follow. For us as individuals swimming in this sea of accelerated everything, we'll need to fashion our own life vests and buoys to keep us afloat and present to the situation as it is. We cannot turn off the machine. We can, however, moderate our own habits and ways of being in the world with our family, colleagues, students and strangers. There is no app for patience. We must grow and nurture and practice our own.

CHAPTER XXV

In Deep Water With Audrey and Tressie

July 2, 2015

As an educator there are plenty of reasons to be on Twitter or to engage on other social media platforms. I'm a PE teacher finishing up a year's hiatus from the classroom and looking forward to getting back into the routine of working with real children.

That said, my intellectual excursions this year have taken me far beyond my classroom and the practice of teaching. Through extensive and very eclectic reading I've ventured into territories that may or may not have to do with education directly. In short my choices have become more political. In the opinions I seek, the analyses I read, the topics addressed reflect a deliberately more politicized interest. So when I do read about K-12 classroom practice or recent trends in ed-tech for instance, a filter I have added is political perspective – where is the author coming from? What factors may be contributing to this person's take on the subject? How might this person's perspective change and influence mine? What I have found is that reading in areas where I feel to some extent "out of my depth" has worked wonders in allowing me to zero in on what my core beliefs and concerns are when it comes to education.

Two authors who regularly challenge me to start treading in the deep end of my beliefs about education are Audrey Watters and Tressie McMillan Cottom. This week they appear to have double teamed on the intersecting topics of technology, education, markets and privacy.

First, Audrey goes to town with this talk given at a panel at the International Society of Technology and Education (ISTE) conference last week: "Is It Time To Give Up On Computers in Schools?"

Provocative? Yes, quite, and by design. Her talk was published on *Hybridpedagogy* [33]. She says:

> Sure, there are subversive features of the computer; but I think the computer's features also involve neoliberalism, late stage capitalism, imperialism, libertarianism, and environmental destruction. They now involve high stakes investment by the global 1%—it's going to be a $60 billion market by 2018, we're told. Computers involve the systematic de-funding and dismantling of a public school system and a devaluation of human labor. They involve the consolidation of corporate and governmental power. They are designed by white men for white men. They involve scientific management. They involve widespread surveillance and, for many students, a more efficient school-to-prison pipeline —

33 http://hybridpedagogy.org/is-it-time-to-give-up-on-computers-in-schools/

Further she suggests:

> We gaze glassy-eyed at the new features in the latest hardware and software—it's always about the latest app, and yet we know there's nothing new there; instead we must stare critically at the belief systems that are embedded in these tools.

It happens often when I read Audrey's work that I am called to attention in a visceral way. Her tone is not alarmist, yet her message is alarming if you dare to sit with the implications of all that she is saying. She speaks to a much deeper question than "should I use Firefox instead of Chrome?" (Which is where many K-12 tech conversations are happening.) Rather, she asserts that our homegrown brands of social and economic inequalities are not only baked into the tools we use but likely reinforce and exacerbate them.

> If we want schools to be democratizing, then we need to stop and consider how computers are likely to entrench the very opposite. Unless we stop them.

Then I came across Tressie McMillan Cottom's remarks prepared for a recently held panel discussion: "New Topics in Social Computing: Data and Education [34]."

Tressie is a sociologist who, in my mind, has moved mountains in the area of public scholarship. Her high profile Twitter account has helped promote the visibility of accessible scholarly writing happening both within and outside the academy. Delving into the broad area of "Data and Education" she asks the reader to get clear with what we mean by "privacy" in this context:

> What if privacy is euphemism for individualism, the politically correct cousin of rational actor theories that drive markets that is fundamentally at odds with even the idea of school as a public good? If that is possible

34 https://tressiemc.files.wordpress.com/2015/07/data-and-privacy-have-been-translated-as-market-issues.docx

(and, I of course, think it is not only possible but the case at hand), then how can we talk about students' privacy while preserving the integrity of data to observe and measure inequality? I suppose that is where I am on current debates about privacy and data in K-12: are we talking about everyone's privacy or are we talking about new ways to mask injustice? Do you get to a Brown v. Board when schools that are also businesses own school data? I suspect not, because the rules governing data are different in markets than they are in public trusts.

To grasp what we are dealing with means that we will have to unpack our firmly held beliefs about what is at stake:

> I question the assumptions about privacy that seem to be the only way we currently have to talk about how deeply enmeshed schools are in markets. Can we talk about privacy in a way that is about justice rather than individualism? If we cannot then privacy may be as big a threat to students as data mining because they are two heads of the same beast.

In agreeing with Audrey's call to rid our schools of computers she remarks:

> I would add: give up on computers and get up on politics. Computers can be fine. Computers are politics. Personalized learning may be fine. Personalized learning is politics. Apps are fine. Apps are politics. Tech is politics. Tech is politics. Tech is politics. Unless and until that is the conversation, then tech is most likely a politics at odds with my own.

So there's that political thing: connecting the things I do, use, and promote to their effect on me, on others, on our collective existence and making decisions about my actions based on the outcomes I say I want. If I say I want a more just world, what am

I doing to support and promote that? How does it show in my voting behavior, in my media consumption, in the way I choose to raise and educate my children, in the friends I keep, in the organizations I endorse and those I decry? Those are political questions, just as they can be deeply existential questions. The choices I make as an individual do not happen in a vacuum. They occur and have implications in and for my surroundings and also express views and beliefs that relate to those surroundings. This is why reading Audrey Watters and Tressie McMillan Cottom has become so important for me. Both point to intersection after intersection where individual decisions collide or overlap with societal assumptions and outcomes.

It's dizzying and disorienting to do this kind of reading on a regular basis. Feeling "out of my depth" comes at a price. I finally understand that "smh" is shorthand for 'shaking my head', but often I am too bewildered to do even that. Being confronted with how much I don't know is not nearly as trying and uncomfortable as recognizing how little thought I have given to some very central facets of my daily existence. Tressie and Audrey take me there and what I choose to do with these fresh insights is entirely up to me. I feel like I may be getting a little wiser, gaining a bit more nuance in my political views, stretching my critical thinking muscles a little further.

Tressie's concluding sentences trigger a peculiar response in me. I think about weightlifting:

> I believe education is a human right when education is broadly defined as the right to know and be. Period. I believe schooling can still do education but it cannot do it and be a market. Information symmetry is at odds with most market relationships and schools have to be about information symmetrically produced, accessed and imagined. Schools can be valuable to markets without becoming them. I believe there is such a thing

as a social category that subsumes markets to societies. I believe those are political choices and only effected by social action.

"Schools can be valuable to markets without becoming them." That feels to me as though a weight has been lifted – off of my shoulders, somehow. There's that blessed moment of recognition: "yeah, that's what I wanted to say." So there's some comfort.

At the same time, "schooling can still do education but it cannot do it and be a market" which is where so much neoliberal rhetoric and policy is leading us: to education systems as markets -there's the weight bearing down on me, on us; the likelihood of freeing ourselves shrinking before our eyes. Unless of course we wake up and see that we in fact have choices. We can lift the weight. We needn't simply succumb to it because it's heavy and makes us incredibly drowsy.

Audrey and Tressie are here to wake us up. And K-12 educators, this is a conversation we need to be in on. Not only listening but dialoguing. This is how we build critical thinking into our curricula and lesson plans: we do it ourselves. Regularly. We wade into the deep waters and have our beliefs challenged. Readings like these provide necessary starting points.

CHAPTER XXVI

Way To Go

August 22, 2015

I happened to read three articles recently which, although covering different topics from different angles, had elements which congregated in my mind to produce an odd, yet satisfying coherence.

First, a pre-school teacher described the conversations among her 4 year-old charges about love and marriage. In the second article a professor of English shared her impressions following a recent week-long institute on digital pedagogy. And the third article is an opinion piece written in response to the Black Lives Matter protest at Bernie Sanders' Rally in Seattle. All three articles were authored by women and the order in which I read them certainly influenced how they have come together in my mind.

Educator A.J. Jennings, writing in a recent issue of *Rethinking Schools* [35], offers a window into her classroom and the worlds of her 4 year-old students. While love and marriage are frequent topics of conversation in the group, she specifically describes the sense-making attempts around same-gender partnerships and marriages within that process. The article really hits all the

---

35   "4 year olds Discuss Love and Marriage" by A.J. Jennings, *Rethinking Schools*, volume 29, No. 4, Summer 2015

high notes of critical pedagogy yet remains fully grounded in the interactions between and among students and their teacher. This is how she describes her use of conversation in the classroom to disrupt binary thinking:

> "As an educator (and a person), I value conversation as a way to build understanding and transform perspectives. It is an incredible curricular tool for addressing issues of identity (e.g., race, class, size, gender, sexuality, ability, religion). It can be especially meaningful when our students initiate the conversations. So I work to create a classroom environment where differing points of view can be addressed and explored. My goal is for the children to feel confident about articulating their point of view and safe enough to consider other perspectives. As teachers, through careful listening, we can identify the issues that kids in our classroom are grappling with. And, through conversation, we can model nonjudgmental behavior and challenge binary thinking.
>
> This is especially significant in early childhood education. As young children develop their understanding of the world, they tend to rely heavily on binaries. If we understand the binaries a child is working within, we can encourage that child to think of counterexamples or introduce counterexamples ourselves into the conversation. These provide useful stumbling blocks that encourage them to expand their thinking."

I am struck by this notion of providing "useful stumbling blocks." That is a lovely pedagogical notion when you consider every learner's need to grapple and struggle with an unfamiliar or difficult concept before being able to integrate it as new knowledge or experience. In a later passage, Jennings contemplates the prospect of parent reactions to talk about same-sex marriage in class and arrives at this insight about her role as the teacher:

> I am acutely aware that my values may be different from those of families I serve. As teachers we live in a gray area—we each have our own ideas, biases, and values, often as varied as those of the children and families we serve. Regardless of any one of our ideological slants, a large part of our job is to help our students explore questions deeply and be able to think for themselves.

Look at that last sentence: "...a large part of our job is to help our students explore questions deeply and be able to think for themselves." Raise your hand if you can say "Amen" to that. This idea excites me. I want so badly to agree not only in word but also in practice, although I see that I still have a long road to travel in making that happen to full effect with my students.

It was in this frame of mind that I arrived at the Hybrid Pedagogy post by Robin DeRosa [36]. Professor DeRosa's work is focused on the research and use of Open Educational Resources (OER) and she served as an invited fellow at the Digital Pedagogy Lab Summer Institute. At first glance this read would seem to be a far away from pre-school conversations by the sandbox. The irony is that the fundamental questions about how to structure conversations which broaden participation AND deepen understanding emerge as oddly connected. While Jennings is addressing the cognitive, social and emotional needs of students in her classroom environment, DeRosa reflects on the specific challenges of seeking to make academic scholarship genuinely public:

> The challenge of being a public scholar is not just in being accountable for your words to a vast, diverse

36 "Working In/At Public" by Robin DeRosa, *Hybrid Pedagogy Journal*, August 20, 2015

audience; it's in being responsible for demanding that the vastness and diversity be preserved in the face of pressure to close it off for the profit or comfort of the elite.

DeRosa's struggle, while much wider in scope, has very much to do with questions about who gets to talk about what and under which circumstances equitable dialogues can take place. In some ways, I see DeRosa making the case for spaces (digital and otherwise) in which the type of exchange espoused by Jennings in her classroom ("careful listening, ...through conversation ... model[ing] nonjudgmental behavior and challeng[ing] binary thinking") might also be possible between and among scholars and "the public" on potentially contentious topics (which could be anything and everything). The vision for such a space exists even if the conditions for its widespread development appear less than rosy. Professor DeRosa offers this in conclusion:

> As Sara Goldrick-Rab demonstrates, public spaces are fraught with danger and stomach-aches... but they are intimately connected to the vision many of us have for the public commons as an accessible, learner-driven space for diverse voices to share and create knowledge.

Imagine that: "...an accessible, learner-driven space for diverse voices to share and create knowledge." What if we could carry Jenning's notion of pedagogy right on through elementary, secondary and higher ed and beyond? What would happen if, throughout our school experience we actively developed the habit of "exploring questions deeply" and thinking for ourselves? What type of "public" might we then produce as a society?

Professor DeRosa referenced the final essay in her post and used one of the major ideas to frame her post's recommendations. In response to the Black Lives Matter protest at the Bernie Sanders' Rally in Seattle, Washington state senator,

Pramila Jayapal, provided her thoughts on a difficult topic [37]. As an opinion piece it provides balance, perspective and rare wisdom. In her concluding paragraph Senator Jayapal captures the multiple perspectives on the dilemma and refrains from insisting that readers pick a side. Rather, she encourages all of us to consider how we can expand our capacity to "call people in" even if we at times must "call them out."

> 5) **Here's what I am trying to deeply think about: How do we call people in even as we call them out?** As a brown woman, the only woman of color in the state senate, often the only person of color in many rooms, I am constantly thinking about this. To build a movement, we have to be smarter than those who are trying to divide us. We have to take our anger and rage and channel it into building, growing, loving, holding each other up. We need our outlets too, our places of safety where we can say what we think without worrying about how it's going to land, where we can call out even our white loved ones, friends, allies for what they are not doing. But in the end, if we want to win for ALL of us on racial, economic, and social justice issues, we need multiple sets of tactics, working together. Some are disruptive tactics. Some are loving tactics. Some are truth-telling tactics. Some can only be taken on by white people. Some can only be taken on by people of color. Sometimes we need someone from the other strand to step in and hold us up. Other times, we have to step out and hold them up. Each of us has a different role to play but we all have to hold the collective space for movement building together. That's what I hope we all keep in mind and work on together. It's the only way we move forward.

37 "Guest Editorial: Why Saturday's Bernie Sanders Rally Left Me Feeling Heartbroken" by Pramila Jayapal, August 9th, 2015 on The Stranger.com

The compassion which enables this kind of response requires training and practice. If we spend most of our time doing the talking, we will not suddenly become better listeners. We need to practice *both*: listening and speaking, helping out and being helped, raising our own voices and amplifying others' voices. There is no single right way to pursue and elevate a movement. There may be more questions than answers and to each question a variety of valid responses. Learning to cope with the reality and difficulty of that variety brings us right back to Jennings' "useful stumbling blocks" if we can allow ourselves to view them in that way.

> If we spend most of our time doing the talking, we will not suddenly become better listeners. We need to practice both: listening and speaking, helping out and being helped, raising our own voices and amplifying others' voices.

I find in each of these essays an aspirational spirit which moves me. Like Jennings I aim to create a classroom atmosphere where questions are welcomed and encouraged. Along with Robin DeRosa I desire safe and stimulating places where I can dialogue and discuss on equal footing with scholars, participants and interested interlopers both online and off; a place where I may identify as both learner and contributor. Pramila Jayapal suggests a 'both/and' frame of social and political functioning to which I aspire and also know to be extremely demanding in terms of cognitive and emotional stamina, particularly in times of stress. All three authors reach me at the critical level of identity, which is where the real decision-making happens. They provide both reasons and visions for me to want to do better, be better as an educator, coach, learner, and human.

CHAPTER XVII

Dodgeball
Discussions

November 30, 2015

Early this morning my 5th Graders and I had a conversation. After viewing and following their self-produced warm-up videos, I had planned on a short game of "Dodge Pop-Up" to celebrate and reward their hard work. One boy raised his hand and suggested that playing the game with a helping option was, in his words, "dumb" and made the game "boring" because it made it too easy for people to get back into the game. His back-up came from another boy who suggested that "all of us" felt that way and this offered me the cue that the conversation was just beginning.

Sometimes our most teachable moments arrive so neatly packaged and this seemed to be one of those occasions. As the dialogue unfolded, we discovered that in fact, not "all" students felt the same way about how the game was played. Some objections came from a few girls who suggested that without the freedom to "free" each other by giving tagged players a ball, several students might spend the whole time sitting and waiting for that single player who tagged them to be hit and go down, thereby freeing the sitting player to get up and run again.

One boy suggested that instead of sitting out, tagged players could step out and do a series of exercises like sit-ups or jumping jacks before re-entering the game. Well, that idea just got shot down from all angles. This is where I halted the conversation and called their attention to what just happened. While the first boy's suggestion to get rid of the helping option was listened to and backed by some, this boy's idea was knocked off the table as soon as he put it out there. I told them that it revealed a lot about who holds power to voice an opinion in the group.

From there we moved on to who was supporting which version of the game. The strongest throwers and runners (who happened to be all male) were in favor of the 'no-help' version, while others in the class felt that the help option had a real purpose. I could not help but point out that the strongest members in the context of this game were speaking from a place of privilege, where the 'no-help' option would more likely favor their position as dominant in the game.

One girl who hadn't spoken up yet raised her hand and began sharing an idea when she was cut off by one of the boys. I had to call that out. "Girl speaking, boy interrupting." I encouraged her to continue and she shared the view that we were talking about a game, which shouldn't be such a big deal. I paraphrased when another boy in the corner butted in. "Woman speaking, boy interrupting." They were beginning to get my point.

While there was much more to the conversation – more voices, more opinions than the ones shared here – the point for me was developing their awareness. We're talking about a game and we're also talking about who we are in the game, and who has power in the game, and how the game makes us feel when we play it and according to whose rules. The conversation was not about dodgeball, yes or no, this conversation was about how we play and what are we creating in the way we choose to play it.

And there's the key – how we – actually they, students, choose to play. What rules can we agree on and how do we negotiate rules which produce fair and satisfying game experiences not only for a few 'skill privileged' but for the entire group? These are the questions I want us to wrestle with from time to time. Because the notion that "it's just a game" strikes me as a cop out, a way of denying how much more we invest in becoming and staying 'players'.

The students finally played and introduced a compromise solution: the 'help' option (giving tagged players a ball) was abandoned but tagged players would be able to pick up a stray ball and re-enter the game. I observed and I filmed them. I invited them to watch the playback. What did we see? They still helped each other and not only the "weaker" players, everyone used the opportunity to help out friends by rolling or tossing them a ball to get back in the game. I said "it's almost as if you couldn't help helping each other." So after our lengthy discussion, it turned out that the familiar habit of helping won out and proved more beneficial to the feel of the game – for the whole group. Helping each other was the choice they actually made in practice.

That seems, indeed, like something to celebrate.

CHAPTER XXVIII

Of Leaders, Followers and the Self

May 15, 2016

'Follow the Leader' is a staple activity in my elementary physical education classes. We start in Pre-K in pairs and move up to groups of 3 and 4 in the primary grades. It's a simple exercise, easy to understand and provides opportunities for everyone to practice both leading and following. Leading is a big deal in the elementary years. Line leader, class helper, door holder – titles of authority and indicators of special tasks can mean a lot to young students. Being first may hold such a huge importance for some students that they are prepared to openly struggle to maintain or capture the coveted pole position. For young children being first is often what defines the leader.

In the context of class lines for example, being the leader involves higher visibility, some responsibility, and likely more attention. Following, in contrast, conveys much of the opposite: less visibility, no special responsibilities, and probably less direct attention from adults.

I've been thinking hard about following recently. In preparation for an all elementary event during which our 5th graders will be the primary leaders, my colleague and I are having them practice teaching games to their classmates. We provide the game descriptions and some presentation guidelines. On the whole, students do a fairly good job of "standing and delivering", as it were. The struggle, however, lies in the following.

I am often taken aback at how inconsiderate peers can be of each other when two classmates are up front presenting. Their fellow students chat, interrupt, and joke around while the presenters try to accomplish a task that will benefit the whole group. (Ultimately, everyone gets to play the game so there's a tangible reward for completing the first part of the task successfully.)

Almost everyone volunteers to lead, yet few show much interest in following.

This is a genuine conundrum.

In the earlier grade levels, my kids and I talk about being both good leaders and good followers, usually in the context of the game "follow the leader." Good followers are helpers; they support a leader by cooperating with her or him. In turn, good leaders look out for those who are following them – they adjust to make sure that everyone can keep up and stay together. We discuss how good leaders are also helpers. Without too much abstraction (and numerous reminders) 5, 6 and 7 year olds can get this and make use of it.

My 5th graders (and likely all elementary students) have lots of other things on their minds: fitting in with their peers, being cool, how they look, whom they like, whom they fear... I suppose the list goes on and on. Their social hierarchies are visibly complex and evolving; hardly flexible or permeable at will. Individual choices about whom to follow, when, and under which circumstances, are bubbling both beneath and on the surface in every PE class. And while we're not playing 'follow the leader' as a distinct activity, for sure, the dynamics of leading and following are on display minute by minute. Power need not always show itself in adversarial behaviors.

On the contrary, many more of the social interactions I observe among peers in 5th grade revolve around pleasing, entertaining, and buffering. When I observe students being rude and inattentive towards their classmates who are leading an activity, what I am also seeing are non-prescribed forms of followership: One friend trying to impress another, a group outsider seeking an in to the popular bunch, the momentary amusement afforded by a class clown – these are all part of the picture. Students' boisterousness or lack of focus is not malicious – they appear to be, instead, the result of various social priorities, which have little direct connection to my lesson objectives.

Meanwhile, in the current education climate we gladly center conversations around leadership and how to prepare students to pursue and practice leadership in a variety of ways and contexts. I get that. At the same time, I wonder if we do this at the cost of lessons dedicated to what the vast majority of us will need to do more of the time when we engage in groups and teams: *follow*. **And when I say follow, what I mean is to be a constructive, alert and active group member.** Thinking about the dilemma with my students and considering many of my own engagements with peers and groups – the need to develop and train group members to recognize their significant roles in shaping processes and determining the quality of the outcomes strikes me as so much greater.

In my classes as well as in my meetings, I want to work with group members who

- manage to listen and think before speaking,
- extend the respect and consideration they also hope to receive,
- can stay open to ideas which are not their own,
- are present with positive purpose and intentions,
- can respect and adhere to constructive group norms,
- can admit mistakes as well as celebrate successes.

As a teacher, these are my objectives: the skills and competencies I want to develop in my students as we go about the business of learning all things PE. My kids are great at giving me the answers they think I want in response to the question: "What made you successful as a group?"

"Teamwork."

It is when I ask them to be more specific that they can, in fact, identify many of the behaviors listed above. They will often mention that someone took the lead and describe how that helped them. Frequently they can point to different group members who led in different ways at different times.

What I want them to understand is that the success of the group requires BOTH: leaders and cooperative group members. I want them to grasp that when they are constructive and active group members who support a shared effort through their actions and words, that too, constitutes a form of leadership that is perhaps even more important: **self-leadership.**

A healthy sense of self-leadership is what allows us to be effective group members – the best possible followers a leader could hope for: supportive, available, attentive and active.

So perhaps rather than cultivate better "followers"– which carries negative connotations – what I wish for is a stronger emphasis on self-leadership in groups. And this may be the term I can use with my 5th graders to help them better recognize how their individual behaviors and choices can shape a group's outcomes. It may be a cognitive stretch at the outset but I feel confident that they (and I) will find space for this idea in our practice.

What We Should Be Talking About When We Talk About Education

May 28, 2017

There are many metaphors we use to capture our ideas of education's purpose in society: a ticket, a key, a vehicle, a road. To describe education's uneven realities we may hear of a struggle, a fight, competition, a race. Whatever metaphor we employ, mobility is often implied: forward, upward, ahead. In the popular imagination, the educated are typically going places.

How we talk about education matters. It becomes the soil in which our assumptions are rooted. We speak our beliefs in the descriptors and metaphors we select. I grew up in a household where education was central to how we identified as a Black family. College attendance was a non-negotiable for me and my two siblings. My parents grew up during the depression. My father served in World War II and my mother migrated north from Tennessee around that time. When they met and married in Cleveland of the 1950's they built the gateway for us to enter the middle class and stay there. If my siblings and I heard it once, we heard it a thousand times, education was the ticket, the treasure, the pathway to a good life we were free to make even better.

In effect, I was raised on the education gospel. In the introduction to her book, *Lower Ed: The Troubling Rise of For-Profit Colleges in the New Economy*[38], Tressie McMillan Cottom describes this belief system as one which views education as a moral good which benefits the individual and society and is always considered a worthwhile use of time and money. My parents opened the door for me to attend the college of my choice and to study whatever I found interesting. They never made demands on me to pursue a certain course or pick a particular school according to their notions of what might yield the best outcome. Although my college choice was certainly a financial stretch for them (as my private secondary schooling had also been), they made it happen and I finished with my BA with under $8,000 in student loans to pay back.

That seems like a fairy tale sum nowadays. Reading *Lower Ed* helped me truly grasp to what degree (!) the times have changed. It's not just that the cost of higher education has exploded in the 30 years since I graduated, but it's that the whole education sector is in the midst of a shift towards increased financialization, corporatization and privatization. The idea of education as a public good is steadily being eroded through public policy supported by billionaire interests from Wall Street to Silicon Valley which proclaim the neoliberal gospel of markets as the answer to every ill.[39]

---

38   *Lower ED : the troubling rise of for-profit colleges in the new economy*, Tressie McMillan Cottom. New York : The New Press, 2018.

39   "Betsy DeVos' Big Education Idea Doesn't Work" by Sarah Carr, on *Slate*. com, Jan. 23, 2017.

Tressie McMillan Cottom pulls back the curtain on how this shift is happening in the area of for-profit colleges and in the process she draws our attention to the social and economic context which makes it possible. She tells us point blank that the essential ingredient for the growth and viability of the for-profit education sector is socioeconomic inequality:

> "Lower Ed is first and foremost, a set of institutions organized to commodify social inequalities and make no social contributions beyond the assumed indirect effect of greater individual human capital." (p.12)

Further she asserts:

> "When education researchers talk about the unmet consumer demand that for-profit colleges serve, they're talking about inequality... When investors and politicians say that for-profit colleges offer a flexible solution to retrain our workforce, they are talking about inequality...
>
> Flexible solutions, on-demand educations, open access career training, reskilling,and upskilling—these are terms that talk about inequality without taking inequality seriously." (p37–38)

If you've grown up with the education gospel as an essential article of faith as I have, it is still a mighty stretch to fathom any such thing as a bad education. Dr. McMillan Cottom sets us straight on this account, too:

> "As it turns out, there is such a thing as a bad education. It is an educational option that, by design, cannot increase students' odds of beating the circumstances of their birth." (p.67)

In this case, education becomes the ticket that expires mid-trip; the path that is cut off by a mudslide, the race you enter that is indefinitely postponed. The most unsettling part of that concept is "by design." Who would actively design options which curtail and constrain the education options of the most vulnerable?

As we are learning from daily reports from DC[40], plenty of people. In a recent *NYT* article[41] about the significant reductions in state funding for public colleges and universities across the country, David Leonhardt wonders aloud about the implications:

> "The United States is investing less in colleges at the same time that the globalized, digital economy has made that education more important than ever. Gaps between college graduates and everyone else are growing in one realm of society after another—including unemployment, wealth and health.

> Given these trends, the declines in state funding are stunning. *It's almost as if our society were deliberately trying to restrict opportunities and worsen income inequality.*"

> (emphasis mine)

Meanwhile, the stratification of messages about the purpose of higher education reinforces the choice inequality detailed in *Lower Ed*. Anthropologist Donna Lanclos challenged this tendency in a thread on Twitter[42]. She asks:

> "So who's privileged enough for us to say to them, "just go to college, learn how to think, it doesn't matter what you major in"?

40   "Trump's first full education budget: Deep cuts to public school programs in pursuit of school choice" by Emma Brown, Valerie Strauss and Danielle Douglas-Gabriel. May 17, 2017 in *Washington Post*

41   "The Assault on Colleges — and the American Dream" by David Leonhardt, May 25, 2017, *New York Times*

42   https://twitter.com/DonnaLanclos/status/867816894937481216

Because that's what employability rhetoric does, it suggests that some students should get degrees for jobs and others get degrees for life"

You needn't go far or ask too many people to realize that we are in a world of trouble. When we talk about education as a motor but cut off access to affordable gas, we are failing as a society. When we hear tell of social and economic ladders to climb but they are only located on the firm ground of upper middle class zip codes, we are failing as a society.

Tressie McMillan Cottom dedicates her book: "For everyone trying to make a dollar out of 15 cents, but especially for the sisters." Based on current poverty statistics[43], the number of people trying to 'make a dollar out of 15 cents' is not shrinking. Breakaway inequality is a feature of our society, not a bug. Our systems of education increasingly mirror that feature while the current political administration seems bent on solidifying it.

How we talk about education often seeks to smooth over this reality. Market choice is not going to suddenly create equitable school systems in urban, rural or suburban areas. More for-profit education options after high school are not going to miraculously bridge the gap between high aspirations and limited resources of time and money for people who are already working hard yet gaining so little ground. Having read *Lower Ed* I feel grateful for Tressie McMillan Cottom's gift of truth: We cannot talk about education without talking about inequality and the impact it has. And when we talk we have to do more than describe, we need to "get up on politics."[44]: Vote, protest, read, inform, discuss, engage. If we have an education gospel worth saving, then 'get up on politics' must be our rallying cry.

---

43 "The War on Poverty, Then and Now" posted by Yves Smith on nakedcapitalism.com, April 5, 2017. Originally published by The Institute for New Economic Thinking, "The Outskirts of Hope: Poverty in America", By Institute Staff, Apr 4, 2017.

44 See "In Deep Water With Audrey and Tressie" in this collection.

CHAPTER XXX

Letting Go Of School In Order To Think About Education

Dec. 8, 2017

On all of my social media profiles I self-identify as "Educator" among other titles and descriptors. I chose "educator" because it's an umbrella term which encompasses both doing and being. To educate others may include teaching, coaching, facilitating, or guiding; providing space, opportunities, materials, structure, collaborators, audience, relevance, push-back and acceptance. As an educator I create possibilities to be speaker and listener, instructor and learner, producer and consumer, writer and reader, expert and novice, role model and seeker, professional and amateur.

When I teach at school, this is not necessarily the list going through my head. It is unlikely that my thinking is focused on the possibilities I am creating or opportunities I am affording myself or my students. No, I am thinking about brass tacks: doing *the thing*, getting it done *in time*, getting the class to do it *my way* (mostly). That is my teaching reality. In my planning I may find the chance to wax philosophical about what I want *the real lesson* to be (i.e., how to work equitably with people who are not your favorites vs. how to play 4 v 4 soccer). Or after the fact, when my colleague and I talk over what worked and didn't work in an activity that we both tried, then I may discover an insight or two about what I am creating or perhaps sabotaging in the process. Reflection belongs to teaching. Doing and acting belong to teaching. Screwing up belongs to teaching. Yet teaching as a set or series of actions does not add up to educating. Teaching is a piece of education, not the whole.

Often when conversations about education get hot, I find that we are actually talking about schools, teachers, policies, students, and families. What schools should do. What students should do. What families should do. What policies should do. We are talking about integral pieces of education but not about education as whole: what it is, what it can enable, how it serves us as a society. Of course this is a much more challenging task. How can we talk about what education is and what it should be when our schools are crumbling, our kids are not always safe (both inside and outside our classrooms), and the disparities between rich and poor are growing by the minute?

I don't have the answer.

What I have come to understand, however, is that we will not achieve better education systems or outcomes without stepping back from the constraints of "school thinking." I need to let go of what I know and think about school—its structures, history, and influence—in order to be able to think more openly about education and its possibilities. And in order to do that it feels necessary to break some rules, to upset some conventions, to seize authority rather than wait for it to be granted.

Free thinking is a political act. Even as I write this, my personal doomsday chorus is getting louder: "you can't write that! Where's your evidence? Where's the data?" That's the trenchant influence of the existing power structure. I have learned its lessons well. "There is no argument without a quote to back it up." Authority, expertise, wisdom is always outside me. To ensure the validity of my own thoughts, I have been taught, I must ground my arguments in the theory and work of other scholars.

I'm going to place that rule aside for now and proceed with my free thinking on education. And my first instance is a selfish one: my own children. What is the education that they will need to serve them well in their lives? I want several things for them:

· To practice being kind.

· Aim to be independent while recognizing that interdependence is also the way of the world and critical to our (I mean, everybody's) survival.

· Learn to ask for and receive help. Practice offering help.

· Appreciate that there are lots of ways to learn things: by reading, observing, trying, asking, teaching, following, researching. Try out lots of different combinations and know that some methods will work better than others for different occasions and goals. Keep talking to people and asking questions. Practice. Get feedback. Practice more. Get more feedback.

· Get to know the culture and climate in which you live. Who seems to be at the top? Who's on the bottom? Where do you seem to fit in? Where can you help someone? How do these systems work? Learn to ask: 'What system is this?'

These are lessons I want my children to not only have but to internalize, practice, in their very particular and individual ways. If I can also help my students travel on and take up these pathways, all the better.

But where do I go with these ideas then?

I start with people. What do people need? People need other people; positive, supportive and caring connections to others. People need purpose—reasons for doing the things they do. We investigate things we want to know more about. We go in search of the things we need. We enlist the help of others to accomplish what we cannot manage on our own. People tend to do well with challenge as long as it does not overwhelm them. Productive challenge cannot be the things which threaten our existence. People require a degree of safety and security in which they can pursue challenge and purpose. Safety and security are what communities build into their webs of relationships through trust and reciprocity.

When I embark on this kind of wide-ranging, human needs-centered thinking, I quickly run into mental roadblocks: not-so-little voices which say, "Be careful! Writing these words, in this way, is risky. It is counter-cultural. It is *against the rules* of expository writing. This is no way to win a debate."

As a teacher and educator, I am aghast at the idea that I would dare to go *against the rules* in a semi-professional setting. From childhood to now, I have been a firm upholder of rules of almost every kind: institutional rules, overt & covert socio-cultural rules, sports rules, you name it. And yet, in this case, I see a need to step outside certain rules, if only briefly, to consider something differently; to see what happens when the ropes are untied and the tension released. Rather than hosting a debate, I invite you to join me on an exploration.

What if, instead of trying to produce good or even excellent students, we aimed more for empowering excellent people, outstanding citizens, valuable community members? What if we created learning centers where people of various ages could gather to pursue purpose, challenge and connection with each other in meaningful ways? What if learning remained part and parcel of living, every day, and we acknowledged and recognized that publicly and privately?

We are so desperate to find secrets, shortcuts and foolproof solutions which will suddenly change everything. Yet, if we have learned nothing else from our extensive schooling titled 'education', we certainly know that this is not the way the world works. There will be no miracles and we need to accept that.

When students and teachers and support staff and administrators leave the school building, the question I have is: where do they go? What do they leave school to go work on? What dilemmas are they trying to solve? What new learning will they engage in, in order to meet a particular goal?

No doubt some of those tasks and questions will be directly related to survival: How do I ensure that we have enough income to keep this roof over our heads? How can I care for my elderly parents, go to work every day and still have a life? What do I need to do to save this relationship? How do I even know if this relationship is worth saving? These are not genius hour questions. But they are the kinds of questions which occupy and preoccupy our minds and instigate a kind of built-in learning which inevitably shapes the lives we are able to lead and create for ourselves.

These are not school questions but they are the ones we will chew on and make meaning with throughout our lives. These are the questions which become our education once we take our rigid notions of school out of the picture. If we want to think differently, even innovatively about education, we need to re-center human needs rather what the "economy" claims it requires. We need to stop feeding the capitalist monster we have so happily created through our highly trained and supremely wasteful consumer behaviors. We need to uncouple "education" from the neoliberal agenda of deepening social inequality. We need to reclaim education as a human-centered public good that belongs to all of us.

If that sounds 'pie in the sky' idealistic to you and me, that's precisely the problem. To change what we have, there seem to be a lot of things we need to let go of. Idealism is not one of them, however.

CHAPTER XXXI

What If?
And What's Wrong?

*Design Thinking and Thinking About
Design We Can't Easily See*

January 14, 2018

Recently I read a searing critique of Design Thinking[45] which likens its spread in popularity to that of a sexually transmitted disease. It's a provocative stance to take and the author offers numerous examples to support his view. I was intrigued for a couple of reasons: my encounters with design thinking have been only peripheral so far and noticing its steady rise, particularly in education circles, made me curious about the approach and what it promises.

I've read about Design Thinking at a distance: in conference workshop descriptions, as part of a Twitter chat, in an occasional blog post. I've even participated virtually in an abbreviated edition. Most reports are particularly enthusiastic about

---

45 "Design Thinking is Kind of Like Syphilis — It's Contagious and Rots Your Brains" by Lee Vinsel, Dec. 6, 2017, on Medium.com

the process, about the synergies created and ideas that emerge (usually in a brief time span of 2–4 hours). Images shared typically feature (mostly white) people talking in small groups or placing sticky notes on chart paper. Participants tend to be smiling and appear energized. It's a process that seems to rely on lots of interpersonal communication and people may have several reasons to move around during the process. By the looks of it, this seems like my kind of activity: engaging, structured, action-oriented, and communicative. Sounds a lot like I how I try to organize my own workshops [46].

In this essay, however, Lee Vinsel [47] pulls back the curtain on the larger game of design thinking. He sees the highly commercialized process as a marketing tool for consulting services which envisions education as a field ideal for feeding that particular capitalist monster.

> What Miller, Kelly, and Hennessy [early proponents of DT] are asking us to imagine is that *design consulting* is or could be a model for retooling all of education, that it has some method for "producing reliably innovative results in any field." They believe that we should use Design Thinking to reform education by treating students as customers, or clients, and making sure our customers are getting what they want. And they assert that Design Thinking should be a central part of what students *learn*, so that graduates come to approach social reality through the model of design consulting. In other words, we should view all of society as if we are in the *design consulting business.*

46 https://edifiedlistener.blog/2017/02/07/speaking-digital-pd/

47 https://medium.com/@sts_news

In response to one comment[48] on his article, Vinsel points out that he is not arguing that all design thinking is bad, but is targeting his critique squarely at a commoditized version of it which can be readily packaged for sale to any number of groups and organizations. And thinking in these terms I can see where my own inner skeptic is activated by this essay.

The versions of design thinking most likely to be shared among K-12 educators as a course or professional development workshop will necessarily need to be practical, meaning that teachers can take it into their classrooms[49] and apply it. The next day. This is what sells for teachers. As a profession we are particularly receptive to answers, solutions and steps. It's most often what we look for when we seek outside help. Imagine if Design Thinking as a process could deliver on what it widely promises:

> The d.schoolers believe Design Thinking is the key to education's future: it "fosters creative confidence and pushes students beyond the boundaries of traditional academic disciplines." It equips students "with a methodology for producing reliably innovative results in any field."

Which teachers wouldn't want a piece of that action? I mean "reliably innovative results in any field?" Sounds too good to be true. And it most likely is. Alas, that particular quote refers to elite undergraduates at Stanford but you know, we could all get there with the right training, ...

One of the further attractions of Design Thinking lies in its future orientation. The process encourages generating new ideas (and products) for the future, solving problems through (drum roll, please) innovation. Most often of a tech-infused digital type.

---

48   "...I would say that I am taking aim at a specific commoditized version of DT, and even more I'm trying to argue that we should NOT take DT as a model for reforming all of education. I hope that latter argument especially is both a) clear and b) true." - Lee Vinsel

49   https://designthinkingforeducators.com/

Intuitively it makes sense that we as educators would want to engage young people in thinking about how to improve things, systems, and services for the future. But there's a catch. The popularized versions of Design Thinking tend to leave politics, social and economic inequality out of the picture. Speaking to that specific dynamic, Megan Erikson provides a healthy dose of Design Thinking critique in her article, "Edutopia" [50]:

> "From the perspective of the tech industry, education and space travel are alike because they are problems in search of rational, personalized, twenty-first century answers, like those arrived at by design thinking. The expectation is that these answers will obliterate material limitations, class struggle—history, past and present."

And applied directly to education:

> "If structural and institutional problems can be solved through nothing more than brainstorming, then it's possible for macro-level inputs (textbooks, teacher salaries) to remain the same, while outputs (test scores, customer service) improve. From the perspective of capitalism, this is the only alchemy that matters."

Erikson insists that optimism among Design Thinkers holds a central role in their ethos and that skepticism is discouraged as it may dampen the 'creative confidence' of its front line practitioners.

Turn the page.

In his book *Nobody* [51], journalist Marc Lamont Hill writes thoughtfully about America's War on The Vulnerable. While describing recent and also past high-profile examples of state and state-sanctioned violence against primarily poor, black and

50 Megan Erikson, "Edutopia" Jacobinmag.com, 03.24.2015
https://www.jacobinmag.com/2015/03/education-technology-gates-erickson/

51 Marc Lamont Hill, *Nobody: Casualties of America's War on the Vulnerable, from Ferguson to Flint and Beyond*, New York: Atria Books, 2016.

brown people, he directs the reader's attention to forms of design which have contributed to the plight of poor communities.

In Ferguson, Missouri where Mike Brown was killed by police officer Darren Wilson in August 2014, Hill provides a detailed account of the destruction of black residential communities in St. Louis following WWII and of how occupants were "resettled" in high-rise public housing complexes like Pruitt-Igoe. Striking here is the way he illustrates the guiding ideas of leading architects as they created housing aimed at reforming the poor. Over decades, white flight, limited job opportunities in St. Louis, along with the destruction of the failed public housing venture in 1972 led many blacks to seek better housing in the first ring of suburbs around St. Louis like Ferguson. In this example Hill offers readers a rare view on one city's development of urban inequality.

In a different chapter, Hill highlights the widespread adoption of 'broken windows' policing in several major American cities in the 1980s and '90s which suggested that the interruption of low level crime would increase a sense of order in particular communities and help reduce the incidence of more violent crimes. In documenting this underlying framework for law enforcement strategy and illustrating how its practice both expanded and distorted some of the authors' original claims, Hill alerts us to the ways in which ideas can become the basis for designing policy. He also shows us how that policy's enactment may stray farther from the authors' intent than they ever imagined. Hill's assertion: "In many places, we have witnessed just what the architects of broken-windows policing feared: that it would be used as a pretext for racist policing." (Noboby, p. 55)

What do these examples have to do with Design Thinking and education?

I wonder about how we educate our students to see the design in the systems they are witnessing, experiencing, and impacted by. *Seeing* patterns of design requires more than 6 steps in a prescribed cycle, while looking into the past as well as the future. Design Thinking aligns well with a certain kind of neoliberal enthusiasm for entrepreneurship and start-up culture. I question how well it lends itself to addressing social dilemmas fueled by historic inequality and stratification. Again, Erikson offers some important insights by contrasting how Design Thinking prefers beginning with the question 'What if?' rather than 'What's wrong?':

> "There are many reasons to start with "What's wrong?" That question is, after all, the basis of critical thought. Belief in a better future feels wonderful if you can swing it, but it is passive, irrelevant, and inert without analysis about how to get there. The only people who benefit from the "build now, think later" strategy are those who are empowered by the social relations of the present."

According to Erikson's analysis, Design Thinking favors those already positioned to benefit from and claim the best of what society has to offer. It stands to reason then those places where Design Thinking finds its most ardent supporters and enthusiastic practitioners will be among those with the resources of time, money and opportunity who can contemplate 'What if' questions in relative existential safety.

In his study of the lives of the vulnerable, Marc Lamont Hill challenges us to go beyond the headlines and video capture of numerous awful human interactions to see the system designs already in place which made those encounters more likely, more predictable, more damaging. He shows us the histories and patterns of disenfranchisement and exclusion of America's vulnerable that are hiding in plain sight. Embedded in those patterns are hundreds of local, statewide and federal design decisions in urban planning, municipal budgeting, school district allocation, law enforcement strategy, and social service delivery all with the potential to support or suppress affected communities. The question 'What's wrong?' is ever present in these contexts but when addressed with the kind of careful analysis that Hill provides we can name the elephant in the room, trace its origins, learn how it grew and was nourished over time.

Our students can see inequality. Many of them experience its injustices on a daily basis. Precisely here is where I would like to see us focus our educator energies: on helping students see and identify the faulty designs throughout our society that plague the most vulnerable among us. In order to dismantle and correct these designs and patterns, they must first be able to notice and name them. That's the kind of design thinking I hope and wish for: Where 'what's wrong?' drives our pursuit of 'what if?'

I also imagine that would be a pretty tough sell in the current marketplace of ideas.

Everything
Else

CHAPTER XXXII

What is an institution?

August 10, 2016

These last few days I've been following the Digital Pedagogy Lab [52] Institute going on at Mary Washington University in Virginia. I tuned in first for Tressie McMillan Cottom's keynote [53] on Monday and enjoyed a "hallway conversation" via Virtual Connecting with Dr. McMillan Cottom, Sean Michael Morris and Cathy Davidson and about 7 other virtual guests via Google Hangout. Since I'm following from my laptop in the living room surrounded by my very personal, yet significant clutter, I've been feeling pretty comfy, laid back, fully at ease.

In between sessions my mind has been very active, particularly at night. After Tressie's talk I woke up thinking about

---

52 DPLI is a 5 day immersive gathering of scholars from a variety of disciplines and institutions focused on topics related to critical digital pedagogy. Participants engage in tracks dedicated to general themes of both theory and practice such as Digital Literacies, Open Pedagogy, Writing About Teaching and other areas. Shorter institutes have been held in Cairo, Prince Edward Island and Vancouver, BC.

53 "Critical Learning and the Corporate University", Tressie McMillan Cottom, August 8, 2016. https://www.youtube.com/watch?v=U8ael-E9fYI&feature=youtu.be

institutions and money. There was one sentence near the end which kinda grabbed me and wouldn't let go. It came up while she was describing the actual mission of her department's launch of a new degree program in Digital Sociology. She asked:

> "How do I develop a space for critical learning while also giving my students the benefit of an institution?
>
> That's what I'm trying to do.
>
> *Institutions actually do still matter. They are one of the ways that we accrue resources.*" (emphasis mine)

She explained that for marginalized folks who do not have equal access to resources, institutions are a pretty good place to be. This made sense to me and mirrored much of my experience both as a student and teacher. I have benefited from the prestige, stability and opportunities of the schools I attended as well as at the schools where I have worked. This thinking also lines up with my parents' strong belief in and commitment to a variety of institutions including our church, all the schools my siblings and I attended, and other civic and religious organizations in which my mother in particular was very active.

Institutions and resources, sure. Pooled resources, shared commitment attached to tangible things: buildings, events, property, furniture...

But something was still itching. I began thinking about now. About the culture we have now. Our very digital culture which is stored increasingly in a so-called "cloud"; the companies we create are no longer "built to last" in the sense that Jim Collins writes about it. Rather, companies are called, "start-ups" as if that's all they will ever need to do – to get started (and wait to be bought). While we are told that everything is open for "disruption" increasingly we need to ask ourselves if this is indeed what we want. So when we talk about institutions – of learning, of social value, of prominence, of tradition, it's easy to create the mental picture of the special building, the rooms inside it, the purposeful people who inhabit such spaces. We can even imagine the habits, rules, norms by which the institution may operate based on our experiences of various forms. We do not lack notions of what an institution is or can be.

Yet linking institutions to accruing resources reminds me of how institutions are often created with very specific hierarchies in mind. An order is specified and forms the basis for how the institution will be run. Of course, then, an institution's original resource is power. Power to make the rules, set the tone, define the group, determine a focus. That seems important to understand. Especially as we speak of disrupting institutions of various forms, let us keep in mind for whom "disruption" is likely to produce wins and for whom it may well manifest the opposite. I find no reason to believe that the power supposedly unleashed in the act of "disrupting" the institution will be evenly or equitably distributed. On the contrary, it seems far more probable that the power may grow or shrink and likely remain consolidated in the hands of the few.

Over a year ago I published a post entitled, "How Much Higher, Education?" [54] in which I wondered aloud about the sustainability of higher education (particularly in the US) in its current set up of exploding financial costs to students minus the guarantee of improved standard of living in the short, medium or long range. In that essay, I expressed this wish:

In my dreams, my children and grandchildren will not go to college; they will give birth to one.

Then that warning wisdom arrives: "Watch what you wish for because you might receive."

Do I wish for my children and grandchildren to create institutions? Do I aim to create institutions? Let's say this. As I participate – as a parent, alumna, employee, donor, board

---

54 How Much Higher, Education?" May 23, 2015: https://medium.com/synapse/how-much-higher-education-653b6b5707c7

member – I am part of the process of sustaining and shaping the institutions to which I belong and in which I have been a member. The degree to which I exercise my influence in different contexts involves choice and self-awareness. Only when I recognize my role and acknowledge my power, can I actively decide to become a force for change or to preserve the status quo.

So when I clumsily asked Jesse Stommel, founder of Hybrid Pedagogy, during a different "hallway conversation" at the lab about Hybrid Pedagogy and its status as, or part of, an institution, I think what I really wanted to ask and understand and explore was:

What is an institution?

How do we understand it? What do we mean by that term? Are you and I talking about the same thing? What happens when we add "digital" as a descriptor? What is different about digital institutions if they, in fact, exist?

My wish for my children and their children is perhaps not so much that they go on to create a lasting thing or things – rather I wish them ample resources in the form of opportunity, fortitude, empathy, and purpose to grow their dreams into realities they can enjoy and take pride in. And the question of what an institution is, isn't, should or shouldn't be, stays on the table for all of us to contemplate and interrogate.

CHAPTER XXXIII

Incuriosity
is a thing

Sept. 25, 2016

One of the aspects of our digital communication cycles that I genuinely lament is the furious pace and volume of generated material. Of course, all this writing, analysis, commentary—it's too much, too fast, too fragmented for us to possibly hope to stay abreast in our fields of interest. But we keep trying. We learn to skim purposefully. We share widely and often with specific targets in mind. We add our own thoughts to the mix with good intentions and this is how the next blog post, think piece, extended response gets written and miraculously finds more than a pair of readers.

Astounding, really.

It so happens that I read an article, a blog post and opinion piece over the weekend and although they didn't seem to be related, there are elements which come together in ways I would not have anticipated.

I'll start with a blog post by Martin Weller which sparked a remarkably engaging conversation in the comment section:

"Open Education and the Unenlightenment" [55]. The post raises questions about how open education should proceed to 'work its magic' in a culture which seems increasingly to be moving away from valuing intellectual output and hard-won expertise.

In a complex world, people don't want to hear that there aren't simple solutions, so the media has dismissed anyone who says otherwise. We can all find our favourite reasons for this I guess: globalization, neo-liberalism, mass media, etc. That's beyond the scope of this post. But it does seem that deliberately, and wilfully remaining ignorant is now seen as acceptable, and indeed desirable in a way that once was not the case. That's my contention anyway, I'm happy to be corrected.

While Martin Weller often apologizes in responding to comments for not making his point clearly enough, what struck me in reading both the post and the comments was precisely that he leaves room for further thinking and discussing.

In closing, Martin Weller states:

> "Education needs to fight not only for its own relevance, but for the culture within which it is situated. Open education needs to ask this of itself though."

This post caught me in an emotional response. I fret for our societies, for our cultures, for our common capacities to peacefully coexist in too many contexts to count. And I agree that people will avoid dealing with complexity wherever possible because it's often messy and time consuming, difficult and draining. And I belong to that cohort. My first impulse in response to complexity is to flee which is typically also not a viable option, so I have developed other coping mechanisms. While generalizing can get you into trouble pretty quickly, what Martin Weller describes based on recent observations resonated on many levels and for that I am immensely grateful.

---

55 Sept. 23, 2016 Martin Weller on The Ed Techie Blog: http://blog.edtechie.net/general-education/open-education-and-the-unenlightenment/

Then I read this piece by Patrick Phillips in *LitHub*: "The Case for White Curiosity: Interrogating the Devastating Effects of White Supremacy in America [56]." Besides addressing his own history of sidestepping authentic conversations on race, he borrows Ta-Nehisi Coates' [57] concept of "white incuriosity" to make sense of how well documented and carefully archived evidence of crimes against black citizens can remain undisturbed for decades. He writes:

> "My book *Blood at the Root* tells the full story of the racial cleansing, and after searching for the traces of those events for nearly a decade, I can now see that my long silence on the subject of race wasn't respectful or polite, as I used to pretend. Instead, like so many other white Americans, I was being woefully, dangerously incurious about the real history of my home."

This concept of being 'incurious' fascinates me. 'Not curious' means that we feel no need to pose questions about a thing or to wonder about its origins. It's not so much that we are against the thing, it simply stays off (not even under) our radar. To be incurious seems hardly blamable at first blush. It invites an 'If-you're-not-concerned, you're-not-concerned' (and that's okay) kind of logic. I imagine incuriosity as particularly tough to recognize, measure or weigh. We don't know what we don't know, right?

In a complex world, not asking questions, not *having* questions, might seem pretty comfortable for some. Maybe the desire is not at all to remain ignorant as Weller's "Unenlightenment" might indicate, but rather to inhabit a space of predictable and

---

56 "The Case for White Curiosity: Interrogating the Devastating Legacy of White Supremacy in America" September 22, 2016 By Patrick Phillips, *LitHub.com*

57 From "The Case for Considering Reparations" January 26, 2016 in *The Atlantic*. It is a response to commentary by Kevin Drum https://www.theatlantic.com/politics/archive/2016/01/tanehisi-coates-reparations/427041/

seemingly safe incuriosity. Because, really, who wants to end up like that cat we've all heard about?

Finally, a third article put the icing on the proverbial cake. The Price of Connection: 'Surveillance Capitalism[58]' by London School of Economics Professor of Media, Nick Couldry, leaves little room for doubt that we've all gotten and are also giving away much more than we bargained for in our use of various digital technologies which populate the internet.

> Online platforms, in spite of their innocent-sounding name, are a way of optimizing the overlap between the domains of social interaction and profit. Capitalism has become focused on expanding the proportion of social life that is open to data collection and data processing: it is as if the social itself has become the new target of capitalism's expansion.

This is not headline news. We're over this, it seems, in that we've grown used to a handful of mega corporations which put a premium on every click we make. And those clicks are used to track nearly every aspect of our online behaviors and that data is then sold to hundreds of brokers. So many things are now so convenient, so simple, so easy that we've forgotten to wonder about what it may be costing us in the short and long term.

After quoting Hegel on freedom as a form of 'being with oneself', Couldry offers this description of our present:

> "Here the self is not isolated, but endlessly being mediated through the world: the world of other things and people, and of its past self and actions. But it can be free if it comes to grasp such processes as its own—related to its goals and not those of others. It is

---

58   "The Price of Connection: Surveillance Capitalism" by Nick Couldry, *The-Conversation.com*
Sept 23, 2016 https://theconversation.com/the-price-of-connection-surveil-lance-capitalism-64124

just this that becomes harder to sustain under surveillance capitalism."

In a world where our moment-to-moment existence is already being tracked and (according to some) better understood by external data-processing systems, the very idea of an independent space of subjectivity from which one can have "freedom" collapses.

What does it mean now when we say that someone is 'left to their own devices'?

As our gadgets continue to grow in prominence and our privacy is increasingly compromised, will we consciously choose to tamp down our claims to free will? I suspect the most obvious and predictable response would be a hearty "No way!" in most circles I inhabit.

But the evidence of action (or rather, inaction) suggests a different impulse. Incuriosity strikes again. It's not that we don't care about what happens with and through our data. Rather, we like things that work and work well. That appear to make our lives easier, more comfortable. That make us feel safer, healthier, and smarter. We like our gadgets and the conveniences they afford. In this state of mind, I'm curious about what's next, what's better, more efficient, cheaper. I am less likely to feel a need to be curious about who is bearing the costs of these 'advances', or to wonder about who is buying all the data that I generate day in and day out and what they are doing with it.

Incuriosity is selective. And that is its most attractive feature. It has a capacity to work in a sort of stealth mode in our deeply human psyche. Free will is hardly free. It, too, requires space and attention to be felt and have an impact. When we choose to fill up on convenience, constant contact, and insist on remaining plugged in, we leave less space for free will to grow. We crowd out the need for wide-ranging and surface-piercing curiosity.

We may not turn our backs on the offer of new knowledge but we want to make sure it comes from the right sources.

Complexity is never going to be everybody's friend. But complexity met with curiosity can become a source of momentum or a point of departure; opportunities to broaden rather than narrow our fabulous humanity. Even as I dare to toss another think piece on the ever-growing pile, I hope we will remember that our power to question gets stronger, the more we use it.

CHAPTER XXXIV

I Notice

November 10, 2016

I notice that the US President elect seems particularly fascinating to adolescent boys of privilege. His bad boy, break-all-the-rules-and-still-win example strikes a chord with many. While none of them would claim to want to grow up to become a nasty and morally reprehensible character (I don't think), for now it's enough to know that a certain brand of misogynist swagger is all in style nowadays.

I notice that there were some people [59] who knew and described exactly that the Republican candidate would succeed and how it would happen. But those were not the voices I was tuned into. I waited with the benevolent believers who thought our hopes would be enough to carry a woman into the position of President of the United States.

I notice that the voices of reconciliation and unity resonate briefly with me because society and a particular kind of upbringing tell me they should. For now they are more like echoes in an empty hall. I hear them but am neither moved nor especially attentive to their call. Instead, I listen for the messiness in

---

59 "Nobody Called This Election Quite Like Michael Moore"
By Shane Ryan | November 9, 2016 PasteMagazine.com

people's reactions. I make space for the anger, resentment and the need to lay blame. These are part and parcel of the human condition. To move along without grieving, without acknowledging the weight of our emotions is to fail the test of humanity. Be all of it and then consider what's next. We don't have to have those answers today. But we can work to know ourselves a little better, a little more deeply than before.

I notice how my teaching, the presence of children, grounds me like no other experience. My students' multifaceted needs to be seen, recognized, comforted, and praised override my momentary preoccupations with myself. And I feel grateful to them for calling me back to my purpose: to be a guide and example for them. With them I remember that I can be whole even if I am feeling undercut by forces beyond their control.

I notice how I read and respond in these first strange days. In a vital conversation with fellow bloggers of color, I asserted that my active voicing of social justice themes in my writing is still relatively new in my life. I am a beginner in many respects. I suggested that I'm not even sure I could call myself "woke." "Waking up" feels much more accurate if I'm being honest with myself and the world. So in my reading, I seek out connection more than content. I identify with stories more than analysis. Few, or better, no think pieces for now. Because all my thinking is in pieces I am not yet ready to stitch together.

These are what I am noticing as I feel my way through these first odd days. Some words I have read and heard which help me develop context, perspective, breathing space:

From my octagenarian uncle in Seattle: "remember, racism is in the water supply."

From Audrey Watters in "Trumped Up Data [60]":

> "I don't believe that answers are found in "data" (that is, in "data" as this pure objective essence of "fact" or

---

60   http://audreywatters.com/2016/11/09/trump

"truth"). Rather, I believe answers – muddier and more mutable and not really answers at all – live in stories."

These questions from Bill Fitzgerald, "How Do We Support Each Other As We Do The Work[61]?"

> • What does it mean to create a safe space for learning for black and brown kids when the leader of the country considers people that look like them to be terrorists, rapists, or drug dealers who should be kicked out of the country?
>
> • What does it mean to stand up against bullying when we have a leader who incorporated abusive behavior as a campaign strategy?
>
> • What does it mean to encourage honesty when we have a leader who actively ignores the truth?
>
> • What does it mean to educate women when we have a leader who consistently demeans women based on their physical appearance, and who brags of sexual assault?

And this tweet:

> If you have security, time, energy, talent, money, skills, or an audience, use them repeatedly and aggressively for good. Do. Not. Stop. — *Jacquelyn Gill (@JacquelynGill) November 9, 2016*

Notice. For now this is what I can do.

---

61 https://funnymonkey.com/2016/how-do-we-support-each-other-as-we-do-the

CHAPTER XXXV

Connecting the Unfortunate Dots

April 19, 2017

My reading patterns have gotten me into trouble more than once, sending me down rabbit holes from which there seemed to be no return. Yet in most cases I suppose it has been "good trouble, necessary trouble" as Rep. John Lewis would say. Today's trouble is tomorrow's insight I figure, so I keep reading, sharing and spinning webs.

I recently encountered some interesting reads arguing for a more critical consideration of teaching and learning to code when it is positioned as a remedy for so many education and employment ills, real and potential. Embedded in that critical stance is a push for ethics as an essential piece of what can otherwise surface as largely technical training. On the one hand, there's a certain pleasure many of us educators take in this narrative. We generally appreciate suggestions which imply that more education, better and more specific training will improve the odds of positive change; perhaps unleash a wave of remarkable individual and institutional advances. On the other hand, we know that this is not how the world works but we keep hoping in spite of ourselves. (And frequently cheering on proposed tech advances to deliver a breakthrough we have not yet envisioned to support that tender hope.)

In one instance I read some good news [62]. A young Latino man who initially ventured into digital networking with the aim of building a mentoring platform for the National Hispanic Institute was recruited to a tech talent search program, sent to a coding academy and is now earning well enough to live reasonably in NYC. His is a definite success story. In response to the question of how his life has changed since completing tech training and getting a job in the industry he says this:

> My salary has doubled and continues to go up every six months. I feel valued, in-demand and confident. I push myself out of desire to grow with the security that I will always have work opportunities and that they will only get better with my investments of time and effort.

And as advice to others who might try this path he offers the following:

> Not to be intimidated. Tech is where we're all equal. You don't need investors or to inherit a trust to get started. You don't have to have started young because tech is always changing. All you need is motivation and focus.

I'm glad that this young man seems to have found a way forward that appears both promising and satisfying on various levels. This is a narrative many of us seek out: individual and outwardly measurable success, a clear upward trajectory emerging from humble beginnings, and as a fairly direct result of educational elbow grease. It's the stuff of the American dream, the one that has become increasingly rare and far more challenging to market as a real thing.

---

62 "TechHired in New York City: Giancarlo Martinez" by Opportunity @Work. org. Apr. 17, 2017

Meanwhile in education at large, in K-12 as well as in the post secondary sector, the salience of this preferred narrative serves as a grotesque template for creating policy which allows politicians to look busy while some students benefit and others suffer the consequences [63]. In the case of calls for increased coding and computer science instruction, there appears to be plenty of enthusiasm from several corners of the education landscape: administrators, parents, students, teachers, policy-makers. The reasoning is straightforward: tech is the future, our kids will need the capacity to code to be successful and capable and, of course, *competitive* in the global economy [64].

Ben Williamson (@BenPatrickWill) takes up this thinking and looks at how it informs education policy in the US and the UK. The article's title: Coding for What [65]? provokes readers at the outset. While Williamson acknowledges the calls for coding in schools as understandable he emphasizes the need for deeper, more nuanced consideration of the social consequences of coding and algorithmic structures in teaching students to work with these potentially powerful tools, particularly in light of the rise of "fake news and computational propaganda."

> "The reality, though, is that coding in the curriculum, and many other learning to code schemes, have tended to overemphasize either economically valuable skills for the software engineering sector, or high-status academic computer science knowledge and skills. There has been far too little focus on enabling young people to appreciate the social consequences of code and algorithms...

63   "Rahm Emanuel's plan to push Chicago teens to go to college, explained" by Alexia Fernández Campbell, Apr. 4, 2017 on Vox.com

64   "Don't teach your kids coding, teach them how to live online" by Kelsey Munro, Mar 25, 2017
The Sydney Morning Herald

65   "Coding For What?" by Ben Williamson on Connected Learning Alliance, Apr. 3, 2017

... There is now a rising tide of concern that learning to code initiatives, like the software engineering sector, may have lost sight of the social effects of technical systems."

Williamson is right to worry. When we present tech to students as one of the only viable ways to advance economically without addressing the ethical dilemmas posed in how tech is used and can be abused and tie that directly to the humans who make it possible, we not only open Pandora's box but steadily feed it with astonishing efficiency.

Even as much of tech and its attendant industries claim to want to make our lives better, easier, and more productive, our stubborn humanity often seems to rise as a barrier en route to achieving those lofty ideals. The fundamental goal assumption of economic benefit as consumer, shareholder, or producer tends to crowd out more complex ethical considerations in the process. Business first, moral constraints later. Much later.

In education we often claim to operate from a different premise. While our articulated goals are many and varied, most relate to benefiting society by developing people. Education in my world view involves growing and cultivating humanity, exploring its diversity and multitudes of expression. In this frame, teaching code must go beyond providing a stepping stone to potentially lucrative employment. When we encourage students, peers, friends, loved ones to learn code, we also implicitly ask them to take their humanity with them and build it into the task. This happens, but the (still overwhelmingly white, western male) humanity that gets baked in often reflects all the prevailing biases [66] which reinscribe inequality again and again and again.

---

66   "How artificial intelligence learns to be racist," Brian Resnick, April 17, 2017. Vox.com

In a brief but fiery post [67], digital consultant, Walter Vannini, insists that

> "It's better to admit that coding is complicated, technically and ethically. Computers, at the moment, can only execute orders, to varying degrees of sophistication. So it's up to the developer to be clear: the machine does what you say, not what you mean."

We, educator humanists, actually wish for precisely that: for the machine to do what we mean. Without, however, reading our minds, invading our e-mail or cataloging our online interactions. Our humanity is complicated and complex. So, too, are its demands on society. Yet our day-to-day requests of tech are simpler: we want things to work, to not cost us anything and to stop transmitting/collecting/sharing our data when we say enough's enough.

When it comes to teaching our young, preparing them for that decidedly uncertain future: which avenues will we promote? How will we counsel them to be productive and thoughtful, financially independent and socially compassionate, to write code *and* unpack its consequences? Both/and propositions tend to be like throwing a wrench into systems hard wired for pernicious either/or binaries.

Guess what our emerging digital citizens need more of in their education: Both wrenches to throw into current systems and courage to build new structures. Compassionate, thoughtful, far-reaching digital citizenship should be the start of the conversation in learning to code, not the add-on. That means changing and rethinking some of our favorite narratives around tech, advancement and education; connecting the unfortunate dots.

---

67   "Coding Is Not Fun, It's Technically and Ethically Complex" by Walter Vannini, Sept. 23, 2016, Aeon.co https://aeon.co/ideas/coding-is-not-fun-it-s-technically-and-ethically-complex

CHAPTER XXXVI

History Calling

December 16, 2018

Although I moved through high school with grades strong enough to have earned the label 'good student,' I had weak points and one of them was History. I never felt like it spoke to me. As far as I was concerned it involved a collection of stories featuring men making important decisions about territory and war against various backdrops of technological advancements, cultural upheavals and religious influences. I could memorize facts and try to connect them but my heart was never in it. I passed tests but only so that I could be relieved of the requirement.

In college, my choice of International Relations as a concentration meant that more History courses would be inevitable. Again, I made my peace with studying just enough to receive a reasonable grade and move on. History as a subject continued to feel burdensome to me—stuffy, long-winded, inaccessible and uninteresting. Studying abroad in Europe and being confronted with historical artifacts at every turn softened my reception and provided more direct entry points to topics I had previously identified as not for me. I did not become a history buff by any means, but I began to appreciate the layers of context for the stories I learned about the city, country and continent I would come to call home for the next three decades.

It registers as perhaps odd then, that my first official teaching job involved introducing 10th graders to European History, from the Fall of Rome to WWI. My Austrian boyfriend at the time laughed out loud when I told him about the job and that I got it [68]. No doubt there was some irony in the assignment. I held that position for 2 years and my learning curve proved both steep and swift. I adapted and benefitted hugely from a team of fellow history teachers who were as compassionate as they were eccentric. They mentored and steered me and by the time I was on my way out, I felt like I had gotten the hang of leading a classroom and not feeling like a remarkable failure. I also had a better handle on how to communicate the broad strokes of European History to young people without boring them to death. Once I was done with that particular assignment, however, I never attempted to teach History again.

Around that same time in my early 20's I had, however, taken a serious shine to non-fiction reading. I held a subscription to *Harper's* which fed my appetite for variety while introducing me to authors and works of interest that I would not have otherwise discovered. It was in *Harper's* that I first encountered David Foster Wallace's sardonic essays, and David Sedaris's distinct autobiographical humor and Shelby Steele's politics of Black respectability. Longtime editor-in-chief, Lewis Lapham, offered me monthly reads that routinely stretched me and my contextual knowledge. *Harper's* provided me an intellectual home before I knew I needed one. Non-fiction reading was the front door through which I entered. When I wandered through bookstores, I would skip fiction altogether and head for the social science shelves and pick the titles that called to me.

---

68 That particular Austrian boyfriend did not last, by the way.

This is still my habit. My current bookshelves are testament to my love affair with non-fiction.

In a sense, writing is my non-fiction love song. Seeking to comprehend the human condition from various angles, I have invited sociologists, economists, cultural critics, psychologists, educators, journalists, business people, athletes, even a few historians into my home to enlighten and challenge me. After so many years of devout reading, I found that I wanted to share my own views. Publicly. With other people. On the Internet. Precisely that inclination has brought me to the present moment: enmeshed in an accelerated and ongoing exchange of reading and writing, of consumption and production, online and off. My output astounds me nearly as greatly as my capacity to read and process freshly published work.

And there's a catch of course. One major discovery is that while I have broadened my reading diet with a far more diverse selection of authors, I have had to recognize gaps in knowledge—primarily of history. The more I listen to women authors and hear from writers who are Black, Latinx or Native American, the greater my awareness of what I have missed in so many books of non-fiction that line my shelves. When I have wanted to rail against trends in popular education technology, for instance, Audrey Watters has consistently reminded me that these trends have roots that go deeper than the founding of Google or Amazon. In reading about accountability schemes in US public school systems and the rise of charter schools, I was confronted with how little I actually knew about the history of racial segregation and how prominently it figured in public schooling. While discovering Native American authors describing day-to-day existential threats to upholding a tribal identity both on and off reservations, I was nearly struck dumb bearing witness the countless efforts at Native erasure applied by government agencies and settler societies over centuries.

In 2013 or '14, a colleague recommended Isabel Wilkerson's *The Warmth of Other Suns* [69] to me and I remember nearly being in tears as I read about the risks and heartache Black folks took upon themselves to leave the South in search of better lives up North or out West. For once I was reading a history that included the experiences of my grandparents and parents. Another study that stunned me with its connection to our family's past was *Reproducing Racism* [70] by Daria Roithmayer in which she documents the influence of everyday choices that lock in white social and economic advantage. Her descriptions of the mechanics of redlining in Northern cities like Chicago and Boston sparked my memory of being told about how my parents' house was spray painted when they moved in as one of the first Black families on the block. Several years later, by the time I was 6 or 7, the majority of the families on our street were Black and the few white holdouts were elderly folks too poor to move elsewhere.

Growing up I could not find a real use for history in my life. I learned that success required looking towards the future and as a family we had evidence that matters were looking up for people like us. My siblings and I all attended and completed 4 year college degree programs. As adults we each went on to lead successful independent lives and our parents both were able to enjoy several years of retirement together. Astounding but true, a generation later and I fear for my children's and grandchildren's opportunities to build lives of their own making with the same degree of economic latitude that we enjoyed. Suddenly and with more than a little irony, it has dawned on me that I can hardly make good sense of the current political moment or its trajectory without a firmer grasp of the historical influences that brought us here.

---

69 Wilkerson, Isabel. *The Warmth of Other Suns.* First Vintage Books. New York. 2011

70 Roithmayer, Daria. *Reproducing Racism: How Everyday Choices Lock In White Advantage.* New York and London: New York University Press, 2014.

Following the US presidential election November 2016, its demoralizing aftermath, and determined to insure that my youngest would at least have a better grasp of some of the historical context I was missing in understanding my own coming of age, we read aloud the graphic novel series *March* [71] by Rep. John Lewis, Andrew Aydin, and Nate Powell. Again I had to own up to my ignorance of the Civil Rights Movement beyond the most dramatic episodes and a handful of famous names. My son had so many excellent questions for which I did not have reliable answers. In parallel I delved into Prof. Carol Anderson's *White Rage* [72] which provided me with thorough background information to explore his questions alongside my own. Rather than hiding my gaps, I was learning to confront them head on. Shame for not knowing served no one. My correction course so far has proven to be a steady and rewarding uphill.

Reading the voices of people whose experiences map more closely to mine and those of my parents has been eye-opening and world expanding for me. A further catch in this process has involved recognizing how struggles for full citizenship—for Blacks, for Indigenous people, for immigrants who cannot slip under the radar of whiteness—are further linked to the struggles for legal recognition and protection of gender non-conforming people, the disabled, the impoverished, the mentally ill—anyone and everyone who may be marginalized by a dominant white supremacist society which operates under largely neoliberal patriarchal policies. So many of my early non-fiction smart reads conveniently sidelined and overwrote these perspectives as if they simply didn't figure. It has taken me a shamefully long time to notice this.

History has come for me after all. Neither gently nor quietly. History has refused to take a back seat in my intellectual pursuits.

---

71 Lewis, John; Aydin, Andrew; Powell, Nate. *March* Marietta, GA, USA: Top Shelf Productions, 2017.

72 Anderson, Carol. *White Rage* New York, NY: Bloomsbury, 2017.

She demands my attention, focused study and application to the here and now. She requires not just that I read books but that I place them in context, and rebuild context around the topics I am so desperate to comment on. We face uncertain times. Professor Mary Frances Berry assures us that *History Teaches Us To Resist* [73]. Although I played hooky from History before, I am absolutely here for it now. Resistance is on my agenda.

---

73   Berry, Mary Frances. *History Teaches Us To Resist*. Boston: Beacon Press, 2018.

Wrapping Up

CHAPTER XXXVII

A Learning Life Well Lived

"Hey, Sherri, how's your learning life going?" asked no one ever. Folks don't sidle up to you and wonder "So, what's happening in your adult development these days, anything exciting?" Instead we ask about how people are—what their families are up to, how work is going. These are our established customs. In more intimate conversation between friends it may be fine to inquire about someone's love or sex life but for whatever reason "learning life" rarely makes the cut. I wonder why not.

Absence of the question does not mean that we are not engaging in learning pursuits. Plenty of people discuss, write, share and broadcast their learning in a variety of forms and contexts, online and off. Examples might appear in the form of letters to the editor, social media posts sharing links to specific content, participation in a community organizing effort or a workplace book club. These expressions, however, may become so compartmentalized in both presentation and reception that appreciating how these same activities connect and comprise an individual's learning life becomes an unlikely prospect. Outside of formal school structures or work related training, as adults we may be hard pressed to consider our learning pathways shaped by curiosity and chosen interests.

With my writing I want to make a strong case for leading a broad and open learning life from the cradle to the grave. A learning life that edifies and delights us, that fills us with marvel and fertilizes our curiosity—that's the learning life I dream of for all of us. A learning life that stands in stark contrast to the neoliberal economic imperative of "lifelong learning" which may sound the same but implies learning for the sake of remaining employable in order to generate yet more wealth for the 1%. No, my vision of a learning life well lived has entirely different aims.

A learning life well lived creates space for us to deepen our connection both to our shared humanity and the natural world we inhabit. I would love for us to be able to hold up our learning lives as testaments to growth and development towards better outcomes for everybody: Towards economic justice, towards inclusive societies, towards equitable opportunities and care, towards environmental preservation and stewardship, towards a world we dream of for our children and grandchildren's children.

I did not know this when I began writing publicly. I had no mid to long-range plan for making "learning lives" a focal point on the way to creating more just societies. Rather, I found that the more I read, the more compelled I felt to process my responses through writing. My inclination to explore new areas of interest intensified as my eye for unlikely connections grew sharper. In concrete terms it means that I have published over 300 blog posts in the space of about 5 years. That translates to somewhere around 27,000 words distributed over a host of topics—as eclectic as you please. Add to that over 35,000 tweets and it amounts to a nice pile of digital debris I've put out there. Yet much of it, the bulk of it I believe, underscores my desire to participate in understanding the world we inhabit.

"To participate in understanding"—it's a desire that goes beyond taking in and processing what's there. It calls for actively engaging in dialogue. Listening and then responding. Cultivating mutual exchange. There simply can be no engagement in isolation. I am certain that my most profound learning gains in these last years have been through and with communities of other learners—questionners, critics, truth seekers and truth tellers. I have found them, sought them out and discovered both their might and their frailties. They have nourished and sustained me, held me accountable and supported me.

I think we routinely underestimate how much people are able to grow even as they age and mature. Learning as a choice activity is decidedly undersold, especially for adults. It excites me that in my 24th year of teaching physical education, I decided to do away with "reminder tickets" which document off-task or disruptive behavior. It surprises me to recognize that this change of practice grew out of dialogue and discussion with other educators about a book we read together. If my teaching has changed much in the last three to five years I can attribute that in large part to my connections online. The readings that I have done, the conversations that I've been able to have, and the conferences that I have attended have all allowed me to discover new ways of doing things that I thought I knew how to do. Those connections have pushed me to recognize that I can change; that it is within me to think differently, to see things differently. As a result my professional life has become so much more exciting, captivating and rewarding because I begin to see my students differently. I see them more completely and recognize how we are in this together.

My shortest blog post ever is titled, "Statement of Intent" and reads as follows: "If I do nothing else, let me curate and share to positive effect. That is a wish, a commitment, a realization, a purpose." There's my idea of a learning life well lived captured succinctly and clearly. Curate and share to positive effect—I'm here for it and all the variety that might entail. As I acknowledge that I am more parts ignorance than knowledge, a sense of urgency arises in me to dedicate what learning energies I hold to broadening and deepening my knowledge base while remaining curious about the multitudes about which I know nothing.

At the end of this collection here's what I hope you'll take with you: a mirror into your own learning life. Although "take with you" is not quite right. Locate, perhaps. Or discover. I want all of us to acknowledge the multiple trips we find ourselves on—not one journey but several—some with set destinations but many without—and claim the learning in process and product as our own, constantly evolving, growing, changing. And rather than get caught up in our answers, I hope most for the expansion of our curiosity. I ache for the primacy of strong, robust questions that take us deeper into a topic and challenge us in our firm beliefs. Let our lazy assumptions be shaken, our little lies of convenience and comfort be troubled and laid bare. Observation can be a lovely tool to begin. Engaging the work of many others through reading, dialogue and analysis expands our capacity to use our learning for good.

Acknowledgements

Writing a book is a dream I've had for a long time. And it is a dream that has had a lot of helpers.

Huge indebtedness to my book coach, editor and main cheerleader on this project, Monica LoCascio, assisted in the final phases by Seb Kaltenbrunner.

Alexandra Thompson, is not only an impeccable photographer, she is also a dear friend who was able to create the ideal images to accompany these essays. Thank you, Lex!

To my digital mentors, Audrey Watters, Tressie McMillan Cottom, Maha Bali, Rafranz Davis, Chris Gilliard, Sean Michael Morris, Robin DeRosa, Paul Prinsloo, Jennifer Gonzalez, Kate Bowles - you have each in your own way had a tremendous role in helping me develop my writing voice, online and off.

Deepest gratitude to the rich, vibrant and tireless networks of educators who buoy and sustain me in my practice: #ClearTheAir community led by Valeria Brown, #DisruptTexts founded by Tricia Ebarvia, Kim Parker, Lorena German and Julia Torres; #digped community including Autumm Caines, Bonnie Stewart, Jesse Stommel, George Station, and many others.

Shout out to my fellow PK-12 educators who inspire me immeasurably: Marian Dingle, Hema Khodai, Jose Vilson, Kory Graham, Bill Ivey, Benjamin Doxtdator, Min Pai, Julie Fellmayer, Mischele Jamgochian.

Gratitude to my educator podcast friends who have kindly hosted me and promoted my work: Justin Schleider, Terry Greene, and Greg Curran.

Thanks to writers Dulce-Marie Flecha, Jennifer Binis, Peter Anderson, Paul Thomas, Angela Dye and Kris Giere among others for nourishing my publication, *Identity, Education and Power* with their contributions and support.

Many thanks to early readers of this manuscript for their gentle feedback and generous encouragement: Craig Jones, Kazuna Soeldner, and Denise VanDeCruze.

To my Uncle Thad Spratlen for commenting regularly on my blog and adding his distinct spice to the conversation.

Shout out to my colleagues at the American International School Vienna, especially my PE team who indulge me in my multiple interests. To my students and athletes who grow and stretch me in new ways every school year and fuel my desire to write and become a better teacher.

Finally, to my husband, Günther, my sons, James and Noah, thank you for letting me be me. My life is richer because you are in it.

Sherri Spelic grew up in Cleveland, Ohio, studied in Providence, Rhode Island and migrated to Vienna, Austria where she has spent the majority of her adult years. As a physical educator, leadership coach, blogger and publisher she dedicates increasing amounts of time to observing and making sense of movement – in bodies, in relationships, in texts, in the atmosphere. Her personal blog, edifiedlistener.blog includes reflections on teaching, learning and the world in general. 2016 marked the launch of her online publication *Identity, Education and Power* which features writing from various authors offering insights on the intersections of those three themes.

Lightning Source UK Ltd.
Milton Keynes UK
UKHW041653010720
365805UK00009B/483